Unpaid Debt

by

Johnnie Davis

DORRANCE
PUBLISHING CO
EST. 1920
PITTSBURGH, PENNSYLVANIA 15236

Dorrance Publishing Co
585 Alpha Drive
Pittsburgh, PA 15238
Visit our website at www.dorrancebookstore.com

ISBN: 979-8-88925-469-0
eISBN: 979-8-88925-969-5

The raindrops fell softly on the hospital's window as the O.R. team scurried to the next patient. Pulling down the bright lights to accommodate the GYN working the night shift, the OR nurses grabbed their instruments to fulfill the next segment of their job. Dressed in the latest scrub styles cleaned and pressed, every worker affiliated with the hospital took extreme pride in assisting the patients to whom they were assigned. In that day and time, there was no such thing as being a rude or disrespectful worker, especially when being replaced was so easy. My mother lay on the table as I proceeded to push my way into the world. Once delivered, they cleaned me off with a cotton-type of cloth, making me bright and shiny like a brand-new piece of silver. Holding me gently in their hands, they passed me around till they placed my feet on a black ink blotter to take my footprints. I was a little cranky because everything was so new to me. The nurse handed me to my mother so she could see my face and then they sent me off to a tiny crib for the nurses to observe me. As they did observe and looked in on me, I also looked back at them.

I lay there in the newborn ward for hours till my tiny belly started to rumble; I was as hungry as ten grown men. The clock slowly ticked by, then from down the hallway came one of the feeding nurses who could see in my eyes that I was not playing, I wanted to suck a tit, a nipple or anything to fill my empty stomach. The hospital had a formula close to Similac for all the newborns, but I needed a little more protein, so they put something else in my bottle. I drank it up and had my fill, then I went firmly back asleep. I stayed in that setting for a few days until my mother brought me home.

I was greeted by my young brothers and sister, who were amazed by my spunky attitude. They knew I was their little brother, the newest addition to our family. As they peered through my swaddling cloth, the thought of attention came to mind; would I be hogging it all up. For the most part, no one really cared because we all had our fair share. My parents devoted a reasonable amount of time and love to all their children.

I was now at my new home on Herzl Street in the Brownsville section of Brooklyn. My mother had gone to the store, placing my older siblings in charge to watch over me; on her way back there was a crowd of people gathered around under the window downstairs in front of our building. They were all gazing at me hanging around on the ledge, they were frightened because I might fall from that height as my siblings played mindlessly inside our apartment. Who knows what I was thinking and what possessed me to go out there alone? My mother, upon returning from the store filled with extreme fear and panic, ran up the stairs straight to the window, yanking me by my little arm and pulling me inside. She began yelling and screaming at the top of her lungs, grabbing her belt, then gave my brothers a whipping they would never forget. Thinking of all the time she carried me in her belly just to lose me to an accident like this was almost un-thinkable. She made them pay dearly for their mistake, one that would hopefully never happen again.

My father was usually at work this time of day in the auto-body shop; he fixed cars that had been in an accident. His pay was good, but it wasn't enough for him to realize his dream; many nights he and a friend would go to a junkyard to steal copper to sell so he could get more money. He didn't let my mother know what he was doing, so she was always suspicious of him being out of the house mostly at this time of night. One time he took me out with him, then he left me at his friend's apartment while he was away. I pouted for a while when I realized he was missing, then I looked around and saw for sure he was not there anymore, so I began to cry unrestrained; I must have been around two years old then. I sulked until he returned; the people he left me with tried to console me, but I only wanted my daddy, then finally after a while he appeared, and my world was okay again. This was probably the one and only time he took me out with him and left me with other people. Most other times we were never separated even though in those days there was more trust in people to watch over your children. In the world we live in now it's not wise to leave your children with anyone, even if you think you know them. Times have changed so drastically since the early nineteen sixties, with more than enough reasons to make a person have their doubts. In other instances, my dad loved having me with him, he liked to show me off to his friends. When he took me to the barber shop, he would hold out his two index fingers and tell me to grab hold of them. I would clutch onto them, dangling for an extended amount of time leaving the other patrons in awe. "Man, Fred, that kid is strong."

It was somewhere about 1963 when we moved to Covert Street in a white three-family house that had plenty of room for us all. At that time, there were seven children who didn't get everything they wanted but had everything they needed; most importantly they had parents that loved them. Times were tough for parents raising children to be nice and decent, with so many distractions. There always seemed to be extra measures to fill in to go along with the unwritten program of learning how to raise your children as they grow.

I had been weaned off the bottle by now, and on this warm dreary day, I saw one on a bed full of milk all alone. I looked around to see if anyone was watching me; I didn't know if it belonged to one of the other children because none of them showed any sort of interest in it. I carefully snuck up on it as if I was a cat ready to pounce, then I plopped right down on it and took a big sip. I immediately flung it hard across the room and spat out the milk, it didn't taste good, then I scuttled to another area of the house surprised that I found a bottle that was filled with sour milk. For me, this was a horrible lesson, one that I didn't want to revisit. In those days, the milk was usually delivered to our doorstep in glass bottles by a milkman which was always fresh and wholesome. So many foods and drinks have lost their flavor and texture throughout the years. Scientists called themselves making better products by developing GMOs (Genetically Modified Organisms), but they only made many things worse. My dad made me aware of the stark difference in products from the time he grew up to the way things were produced around my age. The initial thing that he spoke of was bananas; there were certain name brands, which used to be much bigger, and sweeter, and they held a longer-lasting flavor that diminished over the years. The apples, oranges, pears, cherries, and most other fruits and vegetables didn't taste like the ones that did when he came up. I see that today even more as time goes by, the big companies traded off quality for quantity, to gain more profit. Some have stated the best foods go to the more affluent neighborhoods. This I've seen with my own eyes; the fact is they cost more for the quality. There have been debates about whether all people should get access to good quality fruits, vegetables, meats, poultry, fish, and food in general. This is yet another problem in our society that needs a good sound solution. How these things play a major role in our health and longevity for those who have access and can afford them.

As time moved on, I grew up bouncing around, learning new things, discovering my world, and being receptive. Sometimes people taught me what they knew; at other times I learned on my own. As a young tyke, I enjoyed eating some baby foods labeled Gerber and Beechnut, which were the two main producers I remember. My mother fed me peas, rice, bananas, pears, apples, and oatmeal among other things, which mostly came in little glass jars and small boxes. These were the first staples I remember eating. There were many days I sat by the table being fed that baby food, sometimes enjoying it, other times not very enthusiastic. I guess the vegetables, which may have been blander, didn't appeal to my appetite as much as the fruit kind did (bananas, pears, and applesauce). At times people would sneak in and give me some grown-up food from the table, and I began to look forward to them doing it. Things were so simple then for a child; eat, sleep, shit, and play.

Years later as I grew, I recall gathering ingredients such as bleach, ammonia, and other chemicals, mixing them in a plastic bottle, then burying it to see how it changed when I came back to check on it. Perhaps science and chemistry were deeply embedded in my DNA. Going to school sitting in the auditorium, watching presentations, slide shows or a movie always seems to spawn my curiosity. When the school showed movies, slides, or gave a presentation in the auditorium, those things I never seem to forget. I thought about the world in which we lived and the other people in foreign places; how they lived and what they did to survive. In our reading material pictures of people and their daily rituals were captured. I remember seeing the African tribes with the saucer plates in their lips, the Chinese navigating a junk boat, or in Italy how they traveled Venice on their waterways, also the Australian Aboriginals, who like the American negros were treated like second-class, less than citizens.

When policemen, firemen, or other officials came to our school I paid very close attention to what they said, the information could potentially save lives, at the time I didn't know it but, it could have been my life that it would save. At times the lecture or speech may have been geared toward drugs and the signs of the people that used them. They showed us pictures of uppers, downers, amphetamines, heroin, cocaine, sniffing glue, and marijuana, as well as other things. The one that they didn't mention was alcohol; this was the most important one, but it was not considered a drug. My dad started giving me capfuls of scotch (Johnnie Walker Red) when I had barely started walking. He didn't know the damage he was doing to me at the time; maybe my whole life might have turned out differently. If he knew that he was subjecting me to a very unusual challenge that would follow me throughout my days, perhaps he thought he was gearing me up to be able to drink more controllably. It didn't help though. It only lowered my resistance to make me want more when I drank, launching me into a lifelong career of drugs and alcohol abuse.

When Mom had spare time, she would take me to the school grounds by the school near our house. She took her time dressing me and getting me ready. We walked down the streets as she held my hand, making sure her little man was close to her side. There were other ladies who brought out their children too, and I began to know what socializing was. The children and I found great interest in the swings, which were placed on top of thick rubber pads to absorb our falls. Sprinklers spurted streams of cool refreshing water in the Summertime, while we played carefree and happy. There were also water fountains inside that gave clean drinking water, of which the kids and I would form a line to be next. The playgrounds were only a stone's throw away from our house, so this was convenient for my mom and me. She might stop at the grocery store to get a snack for when we were at the playground. There were two of them I could remember going to before I started kindergarten. Never thought I would be going to school inside the area close to those playgrounds. When I did, I felt as though it was pieces of a puzzle being put together. It wasn't much for many other people to have such an opportunity to spend time with their children, but for my mom, it was a treasure of the greatest value.

In the mornings, my mother would wake up early and fix breakfast, then she would sweep and mop all the floors till the whole place was spotless. Growing up in the South, one had to do chores, which instilled in a young person the value of self-worth. She had friends that seemed to just come around and be a distraction to her. She would indulge them in conversation when she could have been doing her housework. "Oh, child let me tell you now, such and such and so and so, and Kee hee hee." I don't remember any of them ever having a job; they just wanted to come around and chit-chat all day about nothing, like a bunch of cackling hen. Then she would get down on her hands and knees to wax the floors with Dandy floor wax. She also worked at a nursing home called the Queens Manor Nursing Home at night. My mother was a hard worker who enjoyed having her children around her while she was working. She had come a long way from the days when she worked in the fields of the dirty, hot South. She also saw the world change from when she grew up. She didn't want to get stuck in the area where former slaves toiled from sunup to sundown, dirty, funky, never having anything, always relying on the white man for anything of value. The men were broke as shit and very disrespectful; she had to get away from that poor rickety town, that's why she took up with my dad who was a thinker, somebody who had been around. Many Southerners migrated from those godforsaken, downtrodden, worthless places that only brought on a spate of bad memories.

When she was cleaning our house, I was always close by where she could keep an eye on me. At first, I was all over the place until we got some encyclopedias, which became my headquarters. My mother would listen to the daytime soap operas or serials (*The Days of Our Lives*, *The Guiding Light*, *As the World Turns*) and others as the days progressed, while I perused though the books. I remember so many things in the books that were indelibly etched in the far recesses of my psyche; one was that of the Dodo bird who became extinct in part because of poachers hunting them, another reason was it was their time to leave this place, like so many that have also graced the face of the Earth. There were also images of biblical and scientific references, anything from A-to-Z.

As I grew, it was kind of funny that my mother would allow me to look through the encyclopedias, trusting that I wouldn't tear, color, write on or deface the collection. This was something many children did about my age. I took good care of the things I held in my possession though, hardly ever misusing or destroying them as I grew older. My mom told me that she could put a white shirt on me in the morning; I could play outside all day in it without it getting dirty. I would go all week long running around the house playing being a kid, then when Sunday came we all got ready for church. I would put on my good clothes my parents bought me. I polished my shoes, put on my clean white shirt, and looked around for my brothers and sisters waiting to leave. I would stand by my dad and ask him if I could tie his shoes. We all walked in the church as a family unit, then we sat together as others looked on from the isles.

The priest was a White guy named Pastor Schute a very well-respected preacher who helped our community tremendously. When he spoke I listened attentively, but didn't understand what was said so much, but then he would break off the sermon then ask the congregation to give a donation which my parents gave us to put in the basket already. The part I enjoyed the most was when the pastor spoke about the Good Lord. I didn't always know what he was saying or the meaning, but I felt a real connection with the words. When I went back home I looked through the encyclopedias, the stories he spoke about were depicted throughout many sections of the volumes. One I distinctly remember was one of Daniel being held in a den of lions. I thought it was so dangerous for him there surrounded by lions and they didn't devour him; not that they didn't want to eat him the Lord prevented them, but I didn't know it then. The books also showed Moses parting the Red Sea and him holding his staff up with two snakes seized up on top; also, David when he slew Goliath. However vague my memory is today, the time I spent with the volumes was well worth it. Those volumes helped me with the foundation for most of my rational thoughts.

I also watched T.V. with her while she did her chores. I guess I was like her little buddy; I watched *The Jack LaLanne Show* as he taught us different exercises, *Romper Room*, and a few other children shows I can't remember. Once while watching a show, I saw a magician come out of a mirror on the TV into this side of reality, or the real world; I was very fascinated by the illusion. I looked at the mirror in my house and got some funny idea I might be able to do the same thing as he did. The mirror had a little crack by the bottom which I ran my finger across till I cut myself. Mom kissed it and told me to be careful and not to do that again. That was my first time getting cut and it was such a bother; it hurt like hell. From then on, I didn't go too close to that mirror, but I still wondered about the magic man on the other side or things about other dimensions.

Another time our family was bar-be-queuing in the backyard as my dad was hosing down the area to remove the debris; I climbed onto the wooden fence to show off my acrobatic skills, when Dad started hosing me down aiming at me with ice cold water on my bared skin. As I tried to jump down on a safe spot to get some relief from the shock, he just kept on spraying the water till I couldn't take it anymore then jumped onto a pile of trash, I dashed my feet on the broken glass, which gave me lacerations on the bottom of my feet. He sent my brother to the store for first aid supplies to patch me up. I thought to myself, *What a bummer.* I was only trying to have some fun and he messed it all up. When I got patched up, I went back in the house and stayed.

Around this time, I and the other children would play up and down the block. For me, playing was a great opportunity to enjoy my time whether it was in my yard or throughout the neighborhood. We played games like tag, hide-and-seek, coco-livio, kick the can, stickball, Spinning Tops, Skelly and so on. I didn't learn them all as a youngster. I learned them through the years as I got older. There were days when I didn't have anyone to play with so I would be in the backyard doing things to explore. Have you ever picked up an earthworm or caught a butterfly? In these days, I found myself doing all kinds of things to learn, don't think it was to learn so much, but one phase was eating dirt. I also remember at this age I started to get an erection and didn't know why I just wanted to do it, maybe there was something in the dirt. Perhaps the other kids around the area were having sex at a very early age too and so I too wanted in on the action. Didn't know any better, but between the time I grew up as a toddler and the time I went to school, I was familiar with sex.

One of the vivid memories I had was of my siblings and I parked on the living room floor with bowls of cereal on Saturday mornings, watching cartoons. This was a long-standing ritual of eating together on the floor. Through the years, the cereals changed as well as the cartoons. They became more sophisticated.

Somewhere around this time I would start to have dreams; this one was of me flying fighting a dinosaur-like creature. As I flew, I would hit it with a closed fist, but it did little damage. I dreamed in terror trying hard to subdue it to no avail. However long I stayed there fighting I did not win the battle; I soon awoke flushed with fear.

Mom enjoyed taking me places with her, as with all her children. Whenever she did, it made each one feel extra special for the attention. She did this for all of us so there was no need to be jealous. She once took me with her to visit her neighbor next door. A dumb little boy my age stood in the doorway and when I tried to enter he slammed it on my finger. My skin was scraped, peeled back raw on my right index, and my mother became seething red hot. I screamed in agony, enough for her to tell her neighbor to forget about the visit and just took me back home. She put ice on it and told me to lay down; from that day, I always wanted to see that boy again.

Night had fallen, it was summertime, and the air was hot and humid, we had an older type of fan, a streamlined art deco style. It oscillated, blowing cool fresh air across the room and on my smooth toddler skin. People must have worked very hard back then because at night the bedroom was filled with loud snoring noises. For a little tyke like me, this made me think of awful things such as monsters and ghoulish creatures. As the night went on it was hard for me to sleep being that it was so hot, I just laid there on the bed beside my parents with my eyes open staring at the ceiling. My eyes were slowly closing until I heard a sound in the room besides us, I and my parents were the only ones I thought should be there. I sat up in the bed and peered across the room. There on the side by the wall I spotted a figure moving slowly toward the front of the house. I called out to it, "Aye, you" but the creature ignored me and kept moving toward the front of the apartment. I climbed out of the bed to investigate what I thought I saw. As I walked in the front room, I tried to communicate with it, to no avail. He opened the front door and started walking up the stairs in the vestibule as I quickly followed behind it trying to get its attention. It looked like a long, tall figure dressed in a dark Dracula cape. It moved into the hallway leading upstairs so I reached out for it, as I did it stuck out what I thought was its finger and it touched mine; I was frozen on the spot paralyzed I couldn't move or make a sound. I stayed there for a few seconds trying to move but I couldn't until the spell was lifted, and I was free to go. I rushed up the stairs following behind it to find out where the creature went to.

The door to the attic was open, so I went up the set of stairs looking for it. I reached the top where there was a tenant who lived there; he asked me what I was doing by his place. I tried to explain that I had saw a monster and it had come up there. I moved to the side and looked out the window, then I saw a little round flying saucer, which I believed the creature was inside. As it took off, sparks were coming from the bottom of the aircraft. Being so small and not being able to speak clearly, the adults were dumbfounded. Who really knows if what I saw was real or just a figment of my imagination? The tenants that lived upstairs brought me back home and tried to explain what they thought I was saying to my parents. The days that followed left me pondering about the incident, whether it was real or was my experience something I imagined. I still played with the other children and acted as if nothing happened, but every now and then I thought about it, thought about what happened that late night.

My mother spent a lot of time in the kitchen making all kinds of dishes and treats for the family. I enjoyed being in her presence helping her with whatever she would let me; licking the cake batter bowl was my unofficial job. The best part of helping her was when she shared out the food; it was always up to par. Very rarely did she burn food or make an unpleasant meal. Most of the time. she made sure that our meals were as close to perfect as possible.

One summer afternoon, I was in the next room with the other kids playing, doing what kids do. My dad had brought a clock in the house and placed it on a dresser drawer the day before; it was a ceramic horse with a clock built right in the middle of its belly. The other children and I were standing around trying to find something to do. I thought it would be nice to climb up on the dresser and get a closer look at the clock. To get up there, on top of the dresser I had to climb so I pulled out the first two drawers. I started my ascent by placing my foot in the bottom of the first drawer, then the second, and then the dresser started to topple over on me, as the horse came tumbling down. The crash left the ceramic figure in about twenty pieces unable to be fixed or put back together. I cussed under my breath, "Oh shit." My mother came in the room and started yelling, "What in the world? Who did this?" The other kids pointed at me and shouted my name, "Johnnie." My mother came in and picked up the pieces while the other kids started saying, "Ooooo, you gonna get it." I felt bad cause I wanted to fix it, knowing how my dad liked it so much, not knowing how he was going to react.

The day seemed to move very slowly as the pending reprimand left me unsure of my plight. The anxiety was too much so I thought if I was asleep when my dad came nothing would happen. I hopped in the bed and tried to act like I was sleep. About five minutes passed when my dad came home, and all the other kids greeted him as he came in the house. He went into the room where the horse/ shattered clock was placed then immediately he began to yell,

"Bert, who in the hell broke my clock."

She lowered her head and said, "Johnnie."

"Where the hell is he?"

"In the bed."

"You little bad ass boy." He pulled out his thin leather belt from his pants and grabbed me by the arm. He then picked me up in the air and started wailing on my little body. I broke it by accident, but he didn't care. I screamed, "Daddy, no, daddy no, don't do that daddy." As if possessed by a demon, he commenced whipping me till I was covered in whelps and sores. My older sister Bunny, who had her fair share of run-ins with the belt, tried to console me, "It's okay. Johnnie, don't cry." I remained with her at my side sobbing. The whimpers from my mouth were those of one who had been unjustly punished, or so I thought for my part of only being a child. I concluded right there and then that this ass whipping shit has got to stop. I'm not with all that. I had to learn what to do to not be on the receiving end of those awful punishments. I had to try my best to be good.

The next day I deliberately didn't speak to my dad when we were at breakfast. He looked at me cockeyed and said, "You not going to speak, keep on I'll whip your ass again." I looked at him and reluctantly said, "Good morning." There is no question having been beat put an enormous strain on our relationship; though it hurt I had to learn from my mistakes, later I knew it was okay for us both. My dad was trying to achieve some goals in life, having nice things was one of them. Unfortunately, I destroyed one of his prized possessions. One that I shall remember for the rest of my life thanks to that memorable beating.

It was late summer or early fall when my dad started bringing home bricks from buildings that were recently torn down getting them ready for new homes and other housing projects. They needed to be cleaned by scraping the mortar from between and off the sides. I would look at my dad scrape them, and after a while I started to do the same thing he was doing. He would look at me quizzically but didn't say a word. I started scraping them off whenever I saw them laying in the front yard. We would stack them up in the backyard by the side of the house when we were finished cleaning them until they were needed. Eventually he built a bar-be-que pit with a gas line attached to it. On hot summer days we had cookouts; I remember him making lots of food and old fashioned ice cream. I didn't like the ice cream though; it just didn't come up to par, meet my standard. My uncles came over and they would all be jibing each other. One of them tried to come down on my dad for making goat meat.

"Ahh ha, where you get that goat from bruh?

"We don't eat no goat meat."

"You must done lost your mind."

"Go head now, leave me alone now, go head." After the ribbing they would all sit around continuing to drink alcohol. Most of them were only used to the regular things: hamburgers, hot dogs, potato salad, corn on the cob, soda, Kool-Aid, and other fixins. Daddy made ribs, chicken, steak, and whatever else he felt like. When the cookouts were over, they would be half high, almost drunk, ready to go home. My dad enjoyed entertaining and having a good time; for them this was about as good as it got. I can still remember the weather patterns from back then; they were always linked to the memories through the years. The air seemed to have a sweetness to it; when it was hot the sunshine danced on our skins and through the clouds of bar-be-que smoke the food being cooked had a distinct flavor. As the years passed slowly so did the weather patterns. It was way back in the 1980s when the climate started to go haywires; that's when we received the first Indian Summers. Instead of the fall getting much cooler when it was time to, the warm weather patterns lingered about almost into the winter season. Since then, climate control has gone out the window; no one knows what to expect anymore. It seems strange as the climate control shifted, how everything in life also changed. The symbiotic relationship with the planet has gravitated on a de-structive trajectory that is assertively leading towards despair and doom. Future generations may not get an opportunity to come out unscathed by the actions of our parents.

He, my dad, came a long way in life and was happy to enjoy the small things he could with those who were closest to him. As he worked and saved his money he also hustled the streets. He had around three guys working for him driving gypsy cabs. He owned the cars, but they would have to give him a certain amount of money to rent them. Most of the family and friends he kept around him were not on his level.

Every now and then we would all pile up in his Lincoln Mercury and go on a ride. It might be at White Castles, McDonalds, or some other fast-food place. In those days, girls in special uniforms would come to our car to take the order. He enjoyed showing off his family, letting the world know that we were civilized, that we were regular people.

One early morning, we left New York and headed for his sister's house in Philadelphia. Her name was Rosine. They were very close. When we got there, I and the kids played with Cookie; she was our cousin that was happy to have us. She and my sister Bunny, who was older, wanted to ditch me so they came up with a plot. My parents told her to keep an eye on us, but they wanted to go around the neighborhood to look for boys. They started walking away from the house, and I was right behind them. They might have told me to go back, but I didn't listen or know my way, so I kept on following them. Suddenly they were gone, and I was by myself just walking. Sooner or later as I walked through the streets of Philly, somebody asked me where I came from, I told them, "I don't know."

"I don't know where I came from, I was with my family, and we came here."

"Do you remember anything else about where they're at?"

"No. not much"

"Just drove here, from New York."

"Oh, okay."

A few people gathered around, by now I was crying, so they called the police. The officers took me to the precinct and gave me ice cream and I waited. I can't remember who it was that came and picked me up from the police station, but I was very happy to see a familiar face.

The summer has well passed now, it was fall time; the color on the leaves were changing according to the season. Boy, how time flies when you're having fun or just a happy little fellow soaking in all the experience life has to offer. First fall, then the winter and all its regalia, the sounds of Christmas in the air, folks having fun. Sometimes the grown-ups drank beer and alcohol while they told their stories about the good old days.

My parents were from Kingstree, South Carolina, and they had seen a lot coming up. They came to New York during the Great Migration from the South. Blacks left the South in droves to the Northern Cities looking for more opportunities and a better way of life. The people from the South were different and played by another set of rules. They were the cash stacking, money making, fist fighting, stabbing, shooting, cold blooded killers. They were the direct descendants of slaves and their masters, which were at times ruthless tyrants. They learned the most atrocious behavior that was now deeply embedded in their DNA. Though my parents didn't always show the unpleasant side of themselves, we would see it come out at times. My dad told me stories of when he grew up, and the things people did to one another would make your blood curdle. For instance, one time a woman was tired of her man beating on her, so she grabbed a straight razor and held him by the waist of his pants, then proceeded to slice his abdomen. All his intestines were hanging out of his used-to-be waistline as he tried to contain them in his arms, how brutal. Some also used scorching hot grits with syrup or lye to the face. These methods were used instead of the gun; it's a wonder they lived through all that violence.

My dad being born in 1913 in Kingstree, S.C. saw the world change a few times. Racism and segregation fueled the fearmongering and mistreatment. He was not one to buck the system, but he also was never a butt kiss. He a was strong, burly man coming up who learned quickly not to allow others to put him in a difficult position. From the earliest age, he worked for this country's railroad system, cutting ties to make train tracks. As he got older, things got better until the Great Depression.

Things were very hard then; when the stock markets fell everyone was looking for a way to put food on the table. For those who had jobs previously, it was extremely difficult. For the Southerners who were already used to hard living, it was a small transition to stay afloat and survive. They made use of the land and its resources. People searched for a means to feed their families. There were very few handouts, so one had to travel. Hobo camps were filled with the most unscrupulous people; it was cutthroat and dog eat dog. Soup lines formed for blocks long, while the bare minimum was given to sustain the people. Some didn't want to wait online because after they got their food and ate it, they were still hungry. The best thing to do was to get out of where you're at and find a place where you could eat up and fill your belly, which didn't happen often.

As he traveled through the wooded areas, the animals came out to look, to see if a possible meal was close by. While trekking through the backwoods, a truck carrying baked goods crashed on the bank of the road and toppled over. My dad rushed to see if anyone needed help to get out. When he did, he saw it was a truck full of cakes and pies while his stomach spoke to him. He thought quickly how he was going to get what he could before the opportunity was over. He yelled in the truck, "Hey, Mr. white folks, is y'all okay?"

"No nigger, go and get me some help to get me otter here."

"Okay Mr. White folk, Imma goin get y'all some help now, I'll be back."

My dad went around the back of the truck where there were pies, cakes, bread, and all he could want. He started unloading the pies and things taking them into the woods where he could retrieve them when the coast was clear. After the moment he spent stocking up, he went for help and came back. The driver gave him one sweet potato pie, "Here you go, nigger." He looked at him, glad he took all he did. He spent many days in the cold elements trekking back and forth trying to stay above water. Sometimes relatives had food and would invite you in, but resources were scarce.

If you had a job, you were lucky. Sometimes you may have needed more than just luck on your side though to get through this harsh period. If you lost your job there were always people to replace you immediately, so you had to stay on your P's and Q's. Many days passed while looking for a break; no one was so sure about where they wanted to end up as Americans navigating through the Depression.

World War II came along, and the planet was shaken. Hitler was on his mission to dominate with his master race theory. He killed millions of Jews while the world looked on helplessly. The other nationalities wondered if they were next; where would it end? Hitler was a ruthless tyrant that shook the world to its core. He saw what the world was made of by using fear and white supremacy to commit atrocious acts unparalleled throughout history. The whole world wanted to stop him, but only with the help of African Americans and other nations assisting our armed forces were we able to change the outcome of World War II. Blacks fought on the front lines tooth and nail only to come back to a society that treated them as less than, unequal to their white counterparts. Blacks enjoyed more freedom in Europe and abroad than in this country. The American Dream was only afforded to other nationalities that drifted to our shores, while the so-called dream was the American Nightmare for most blacks here.

My dad enlisted in the Merchant Marines traveling throughout Europe and the rest of the world. He certainly could have his fill to eat in there, but he had to be humble and learn to take orders. Before he left, he was somewhere in the South when he got in trouble. He was having sex with young white girls and being a badass. The people from his town wanted to teach him a lesson; so, they locked him up in the jailhouse while he waited to be prosecuted. He asked one of his friends to bring him some matches and some food. When the girl came to visit, she gave it to him then he waited for the right moment. He started a big fire burning down the jail, escaping into the night. He ran for a long while and didn't stop running for fear of being caught. He didn't rest lightly anymore until he enlisted in the Merchant Marines.

His first days on the sea were horrible and unforgiving; he puked everywhere not being able to hold down his food. Then when he was cured of sea sickness he started to work in the kitchen. The ship had a lot of people who were from different parts of the states. Some of the guys thought they were better than him trying to belittle him and make his life miserable. My dad thought about what he was going to do then waited to take action. The guy who had been messing with him went into the bathroom to take a shit. When he did, it was a big mistake. My dad slipped into the little confined area and began to beat him down with a hard piece of oakwood. He pummeled him, leaving him bloody with his excrement sliding all down the side of his clothes. He left him there to clean himself off while he went back to work. From then on they had a perfect understanding.

Next, one of the Stewards that came to the mess hall every afternoon kept complaining about the soup always being cold. My dad was flustered seeing this guy, knowing that he had the same miserable antic. He would come in, sit down and order soup which would be hot when he brought it to the table. He would then sit reading his newspapers until the soup got cold. Then he would look at my dad like he was stupid and claim his soup wasn't hot enough. My dad always had to take it back to the kitchen and bring him another. He spoke to the First Mate about the issue, an older white guy who had been on this ship forever. His eyes were small and beady clouded from cataracts. Then the First Mate told him to put one of the serving bowls in the kitchen's oven overnight. When he brings the soup to him make sure it's boiling hot before he puts it in the bowl and serves it to him. When he did what he was told to do, the Steward took his time as usual, then put it in his mouth and tried to swallow a spoonful. He immediately spewed it across the room, his arms flailing gasping for air, while my dad was in the back watching furtively. That was the last time he remembered him complaining about the soup.

After being at sea for months at a time, Pop was used to furloughs in exotic ports. He and a few other men would get off the ship to have some fun. They didn't mind paying for a good time, but they had to be mindful of their obligations, just hit it and quit it. The ship was anchored somewhere in Europe; the captain told everyone not to leave and stay aboard the ship. My dad couldn't wait any longer to find some nice lady to release his tension. After he left, the ship took a hit; it was sunk leaving no survivors. My dad was a lucky man that day. He saw it as a sign. When he went back to the States, he decided he wanted to leave the Merchant Marines.

He remained in the South for a while where he met my mother. She was in the field sharecropping with other family members when he first saw her. She was a young light-skinned, high yellow gal with desirable features. If you were black or dark-skinned, the lighter the woman you were with meant something. My dad told me it helped our race, so far as features and complexion. I only know my mother was the best, most kind, loving, caring person I ever knew. She was my everything, so sweet, God bless her. She had my oldest brother before my dad met her. Then he came around, a good looking handsome young man who my grandmother thought he would be a good match for her. They started talking for a while then my grandmother gave her approval, she didn't want her to get stuck with the lot of slim pickings. They were married and my dad brought her to New York. This is where the rest of my brothers and sisters were born.

In the early 1960s he and my mother were raising seven head of children in a racist, segregated society. The civil rights movement was still being forged through the courage of Martin Luther King and other activists trying to make things better for the American Negroes. The cost was great, and it took its toll on everyone. There were so many obstacles to freedom that although things have gotten better, they still do exist today.

The sparkle of lights glittering throughout the house, the smells of pine, fruits nuts and candy permeated our senses. Everyone was filled with merriment anticipating Christmas Day, thinking of the gifts that Santa would bring and the joy on the kids' faces when they opened their presents. My mom made her delightful cakes and pies, and my dad helped with preparing the rest of the holiday meals. There was turkey, ham, potato salad, rice and peas, macaroni, candied yams and whatever else that would fit on the table. The food set-up was like this for both Thanksgiving and Christmas. We lived pretty good and ate well for the rest of the year, but these were two traditional dinners that called for going the extra mile. As for me it was fun, because I got to learn, eat, and help out all at the same time, how nice?

The next day we all woke and proceeded for the living room where all the toys and goodies were. I didn't know that Christmas was all about the birth of Jesus Christ. I only knew every year about this time this ritual played out. Later in my life, I began to feel a more spiritual connection when I began to understand what it stood for. So, this year I received a burgundy bike with training wheels, I liked it and couldn't wait to play with it. There were other presents that made everyone happy, but for me the bike was the only one I needed. We all played with our brand-new toys until we were tired, then we started to leave the living room one by one. It didn't seem like a whole lot of things to do for children except play with each other. At the end of the day, I really enjoyed taking a bath. The most frequently used soap by our family was named Ivory. When I went to stay with my aunt Mary, she bought me another brand called Mr. Bubbles. She and my uncle Bob treated me as if I was their very own. They never had children, so I was the next best thing. I stayed with them at periods in my early childhood, which was convenient for my parents. They had more than enough children to deal with. My aunt was kind of strict and mean. Once while sitting at the table waiting to be fed, I said to another, "You're full of bologna."

My aunt Mary said, "What'd you say?"

"I said you're full of" Pow, she slapped the shit out of me. From that day on I vowed to keep an eye on her. Many days after that when I stayed with her, she was working at my school as a monitor or something not too relevant. She had gotten wind that I was acting up in class, the usual acting a fool, being a Joker. So, one day she eased in my class and confronted the teacher, "Does he always act up in here?" The teacher, who did not really want to say too much bad things about me, slightly agreed. Then my aunt Mary pulled out a Hot Wheels track and began to whip me in front of the class. She was determined to make me cry, but I refused to give her the satisfaction. She began to huff and puff till I wore her out. I looked at her like she was crazy. She gathered her things and went dragging her ass down the corridor. When I went back to her house I was thinking it was time to leave, but I didn't though. I basically withdrew my affection for her. Then I learned she had cancer. She would hark spit in a big can she had; she still smoked cigarettes and drank liquor while she was diagnosed. Her status was terminal, and I felt slight remorse. Perhaps her beating me in front of the class was the straw that broke the camel's back. I been in school for a while now still trying to learn all the lessons and etiquette of growing up. This wasn't how it was in kindergarten, but I had to learn from my mistakes.

Kindergarten

On the first day my mom stayed with me for a while till I became acclimated to the other children in my class. We started talking to each other and that broke down barriers. I looked around and we were all having fun so that was all right with me. Throughout the day the teacher gave us directions and we all followed whatever she said. Then came the time for lunch, she showed us our places to be. Then they passed out these little trays of food. I looked at it and was curious about the taste and texture. When I tasted the food, it was almost perfect. The only way it could have been better was if my mom made it herself. For that moment I was hungry, and it didn't really matter to me. So, after we ate and cleaned off the tables, we had to take a nap. The teacher played soft instrumental sounds that promoted sleep, and we dozed off. Forty minutes or so she was walking around placing materials for everyone's desk to retrieve when she gave the signal. The lights were slowly brightened, and she began to talk again, "children there's some material by your desk, pick it up and get ready for the next exercise." The learning was constant and varied. One moment we might be looking at a slide show, then finger painting, then singing exercises, and a variety of things to help us learn different ways. By the end of the day, we were all tuckered out. When I went home, I began to tell my mother of all the things I had done in school that day, and she was so proud. I was very happy to go to school every day now enjoying the fun of being a kid.

After going to the school for a long while the kids were ordered to get vaccination shots for childhood diseases. There had been some outbreaks that concerned the government; they told the parents if they wanted their kids to go to school, they either get them vaccinated or they won't be able to attend. Parents didn't have a problem with getting their children vaccinated, and we avoided many catastrophes. While we were waiting in line, a boy kept crying aloud, which became intolerable to a degree. I wanted to pop him so bad. I can't figure out why he annoyed me so much, I just knew I had to get out of there. When we finally did start on our way back home, my mom bought us a hot dog. We ate it and gave thanks.

About another year had passed and I graduated from kindergarten to the first grade. The seats were bigger, and the classroom looked much different from earlier. There was a partition in the back of the class for us to hang up our coats and store some of our other belongings. In the front of the classroom there was a huge chalkboard that went from one end of the front wall to the other, except for a few feet. When we settled in on the class the teacher instructed us what we would be doing. Then she began to write the alphabet and called them out as she wrote them, "Now this is A, and this is B," till she went up to M. About the first ten, she would ask everyone to repeat after her, and we did whatever she asked. I thought that was so much fun, to be able to read something as the teacher taught us. Now I could go back home and tackle some of those big words in the encyclopedias. In time I would understand what those words meant and be able to appreciate what was being said. The initial way we started to learn was a slow monotone. See Spot run, no Sally stay, Stop Jim, Jack will run with Bill, they all walked home from there. That was probably how they were taught, so that's how they taught us. It wasn't till my latter years in school that I felt like I was not getting the best education my classes had to offer.

I continued to do well throughout the years; between learning and play fighting, I was having a ball. Some days I'd go to the playground lay on my back and look up at the many clouds in the sky and imagine what they could be. The color was usually a spacious sky blue, with puffs of cotton white dancing any which way. I would also play games that required a lot of running around; it was okay because I rarely got tired. At some point, the other kids perceived me as a bully though because I enjoyed fighting, they would begin to avoid me when they saw me coming, I didn't like them being afraid of me. Usually, we played around for lunch and after school for a while before we went home. I needed them to play with me and to have fun. I was about six then, and I could go home by myself;

back then it was all right for a child to go to and from school alone without fear of being accosted by strangers. Later, in time though, I might have heard of some poor child who didn't make it home, or who was abducted, but it was very rare. This also invoked a fear of the unknown.

I recall somewhere around this age I went away to visit a white family in Hawthorne, NY, near White Plains. My mother had brought me some nice new clothes from a department store; I remember mostly because of the unique smell indicative of brand-spanking new things that they sold. We went into department stores picking out outfits that I was to wear while I was away. I was not told yet I was to stay with people I didn't know; it was gradually explained or released to me as time went by. The fresh scent of the brand-new items from a store was a smell I learned to enjoy. It was mostly in big department stores that brought on a sensory awareness, not every store made me feel the same.

After we had shopped and brought enough items to fill my small suitcase, I waited on the day I would leave. It was on a summer day when my mother took me to a bus station. There were other children waiting for departures as well, and we all sat patiently waiting for the signal. They called the individuals by their name, and they were loaded onboard the buses. When I arrived at my destination, there was a white couple that came to greet me. They took me home with them where they had a boy about my age to play with. The first day we played outside with some of his toys; he had big yellow-and-black Tonka trucks for construction. During my stay, there was a parade that passed through the town. The marionettes twirled their batons while the guys played the glockenspiels. The whole town came out and viewed the enjoyable moment. Me and the little boy played in the backyard with his toys as we overlooked the granite quarry. The days passed quickly as we had our fun. The father barbequed some franks and hamburgers for us, which was a treat; the mom made corn fritters that were scrumptious, I had a few before we went asleep. I was also given something to drink at bedtime, which I didn't know would be a problem. Later that night, I relieved myself on the sheets and was surprised, I didn't do that at home. This was the first time I could remember wetting the bed. They gave me something else to drink another day before bedtime, and I did it again. I was frustrated. Soon after that, I was on the next bus back home; they abruptly cancelled my stay. This must have caused the family quite a bit of anxiety; back at home, if a child wets the bed we might just change the sheets and or flip the bed around, with them I think they threw the mattress out.

The next year I went to another family in Montpelier, Vermont. The St. Johns family was also a white family, but they had a lot more children. They had two boys around my age, Dale, and David, along with three girls, Teresa, Paulette they were younger and Coleen. Me and the boys would sleep in a room on the second floor with the windows open for air conditioning. They were nice to me, treating me as one of their own. As I was not from the country but a city dweller, they always showed me their country ways. We walked bare-footed, climbed trees, picked, and ate fresh vegetables from the neighbor's gardens, and walked through their neighborhood. Sometimes when other white people saw me with them, they looked a little longer almost staring, but no one ever said anything, especially the N word. Sometimes David and I would wrestle, and he seemed to always win. I thought because I was black I should have won, but not so; he was better at it than I.

One day we went to a log cabin in the woods, it belonged to one of their close friends named Avery. We stayed there for a few days enjoying living off the land. Mr. St. John brought part of his gun collection with him; he had an arsenal of both guns and rifles. He let me shoot the 22. Cal pistol, and his 22. long-barreled rifle: I aimed at some beer cans he lined up for me and I hit them. Then the children and I would go foraging for blueberries in the meadowlands barefooted. Once we saw a snake and Dale whacked it with a stick, releasing the contents of its belly. It appeared to be pregnant, but we didn't care. None of us liked snakes. We also found wild mushrooms and other food items. As the day moved slowly on, we always seemed to be having fun doing whatever. As we picked the blueberries from the meadowlands or the field, the birds were in abundance chirping, singing, and calling to one another. Each had a distinct sound for its species. Sometimes I tried to mimic them, but they were not always easy to imitate. There were plenty of insects that were scurrying about trying not to be eaten, mostly tending to their individual daily affairs. I couldn't get my fill of being with them. It was nothing like being back in the city. One night I remember the older sister Colleen and her boyfriend taking me to the race car derby. The cars smashed into each other. I was concerned for the driver's safety, but they explained to me in more detail how the drivers were safe. After the derby, they had a real race for the other cars that had to cross the finish line to win the prizes. The night slowly passed until it was time to go. By then it had gotten cool outside, and they gave me a jacket to keep warm. On the way in, we stopped at a Kentucky Fried Chicken to get a fresh hot bucket. It was scrumptious and above the average take-out. When we got back to the house, they took me upstairs where the other children slept and placed me in one of their beds.

The next morning, we made cinnamon toast for breakfast. We combined sugar, cinnamon, and butter and spread it on toast. Later, we worked on some plastic model cars. Also, they had a few big Jig-saw puzzles we put together. Every now and then we would go to the grocery store, and they would buy me a chocolate fudge sickle. I really enjoyed my time with them all, they were just so pleasant. This was all made possible by the courtesy of the Fresh Air Fund. I went back the next year, and we had fun all over again, then on the third year the family moved away. When I arrived back in Vermont, I was saddened to know they had moved from Montpellier. I stayed with another couple that summer, but it was just not the same. When I left there and went back home, I never made it back to that town.

One of my fondest memories with them, they loaded up the family wagon and drove all the way to Canada. We were going to the Granby Zoo, which is in Southwestern Quebec, east of Montreal. Initially, I noticed the roads and streets as we drove, they were immaculate like nothing I'd ever seen. The air was also fresh like Vermont and the people spoke French. We stopped by the U.S. border before we entered the country and the security noticed I was a black child traveling with a white family; they looked in the vehicle asked a few questions and told us to enjoy our stay, but they never asked anything about me. I was a little surprised they didn't. When we left the border we went to a supermarket and bought some cold cuts for sandwiches. The store took American currency which had a slightly higher value than the Canadian, but it wasn't too hard for them to figure out the difference, probably because they exchange money all the time.

We drove a little while further till we reached the zoo. I had been to the animal enclosure in Prospect Park before, and the Bronx Zoo on a school trip when I was in fifth grade but, it was no comparison to the Granby. There were many attractions all throughout the location, however, the one that stood out the most for me was the birds or the Flamingo's. We stayed there for a bit, then we started on our way back to the house. It was a fine day, which gave us all a thrill being close to nature with the unforgettable scents of the animals.

On another occasion while we were back at the shack with Oakey, Papa St. John and Oakey had caught some fish from one of the streams I believe they were rainbow trout. They had cleaned the fish by the water and pulled out a big frying pan. They filled it with oil and was ready to fry but they had no flour. One of them suggested that they use some crumbled-up soda crackers to bread and season the fish. When they finished frying them, they were so tasty and unforgettable. From that day I developed a deep sense of improvisation. Thank you guys for the lifelong lesson.

The seasons changed with precision, it was warm when it was supposed to be and cold when it was winter. I walked home without my coat on at times throwing snowballs, one thing I enjoyed was the cold weather. I also observed the colors of the leaves changing, and their falling to the ground when Autumn came. Every day brought on a new learning experience growing up in the city. It was Christmas time again, and I had gotten a little older. My dad had come home early that day and saw me riding my bike. It still had the training wheels on it, and he told me to hold on for a minute. I stopped and waited for him, then he explained that he was going to teach me how to ride without those training wheels. He said he was going to grab the bike from behind and for me not to stop peddling, just keep going. He grabbed the bike and began to run with me and the bike. I thought he was running well for an older man; he must have been in his upper forties and still had his stamina. He took off and before I knew it, we were flying down the street; I peddled hard and when I looked around my dad was not behind me. I went to the corner and turned around without stopping and that's how I learned to ride my bike, I was ecstatic.

Many days I would come home from school, do my homework, and ask permission to go outside to ride my bike. I mostly rode from corner to corner staying on our block where those who knew me would be able to keep an eye on me. I played with and talked to the other kids while I was outside however I think I was wrapped in my own world. While I was riding my bike, I didn't really need others to enjoy myself, it was all the fun I needed. I took care of my bike for a long while as I did with most of my possessions. Taking care of my belongings helped me to appreciate the things I did have.

Christmas time had come again, and all the presents were laid under the tree. The usual ornaments and light displays were prevalent throughout the house. My siblings were gathered in the living room waiting for their presents to be handed to them. My dad handed them out patiently as I watched on by the side of the back wall. I kept looking at a bike waiting to see who was going to get it, my dad just continued handing out the presents until I had to ask him, "Aye dad, who is that bike for?"

"That's for you, son." He stood up, reached over, grabbed the bike, and handed it to me. Words could hardly express the joy I felt at that moment. I was so grateful.

"Thanks, Dad." With the biggest smile on my face, he knew I was so happy. Somebody adjusted the seat for me, and I went riding as soon as I put on my clothes. It was still a little cool outside but that didn't really bother me; I was just so happy to have my bike and ride it. I stayed out for a while and then I brought it back to the house. This was an eventful Christmas; one I will never forget.

Months passed; and on this early Sunday morning, my dad asked my mother to wake up my brother's friend Renee who had spent the night over and send him home. My mother was reluctant because she wanted to feed him before he left; she didn't say it but that's what she wanted to do. Anyway, my dad had went to another part of town and came back home to find the child still there, and this infuriated my dad. He began to yell that my mother doesn't want to listen, and two minutes later he took a frying pan and bashed her in the forehead. She was bleeding from the wound, whimpering, crying holding her head. We were all very startled, not sure what we should do, the shock hit us all at once in different ways. What a way for a child to grow up with their parents at odds with each other. Things had been brewing for a while, my mom was expecting my dad to be more respectful, loving, and caring when they got married. After they first met he was so attentive, promising her the world which she felt was special. He was clearly frustrated things weren't going his way. The biggest thing he felt was he didn't want to take care of somebody else's children. My mother had a big heart, but my dad told me that he had a hard enough time taking care of his own family and my mom wanted to feed the world. Eventually things came to a head and begun to go downhill. He wanted my mother to be more subservient, for her to just obey whatever he said without question. They used to go out on the town to clubs for a while, but this didn't last; for one my mother wasn't a drinker, and she didn't know how to navigate in that environment. He told me that she would be putting him down in the company of his friends, and they would have a laugh at his expense. Eventually, he stopped taking her out. He was also controlling; when my mom got paid from her job he would ask her for her money to pool with his to pay the bills. On the same note he was having sex with her friends behind her back. She was getting done wrong all the way around the board. Guys from the South seemed to think that they could intimidate their women and treat them any kind of way. Eventually she was fed up suffering in her own world, just holding it all in.

My dad had been stealing copper from a junkyard for a while, and his funds were now sufficient with the money she gave him to buy another house. My parents looked at another place on Greene Ave in the Bushwick section and soon they bought it. When my mom arrived on the scene, she went into the yard and began to clean up the weeds and made it more presentable; the neighbors were watching through their windows when they began to mend the fence. This type of activity may have moved my mother deep within because she was from the South and grew up close to the plants, trees, and meadowlands. Many people from the South that have roots in slavery know how to tend to their plants, take care of their possessions and cook well. After she cleaned the grounds, planted some grass seeds, and a few other kinds of vegetation.

The house was a source of mystery for me as I first started to explore it. By the entrance of the house was a big iron safe that was very heavy, with no money inside of course. It looked like it could have been for a big company that used it to hold large amounts of money. It was open for a long while until someone locked it accidentally while the combination was yet unknown. It stayed in the front of the house for many years before it was finally discarded.

We had just moved in and one of the cardboard boxes had a family of mice stowed away inside. My dad took it outside and poured a flammable liquid over them, maybe turpentine, and lit them on fire. I looked on as they squeaked and reeled from the pain. I was amazed, shocked even for this to have happened, I thought they should have lived, not killed; I guess that was the level of disdain my dad had for the creatures. I felt kind of bad for them because they never had a chance, but that was now a part of life. In the days that followed we became acclimated to the house and the many mysteries it held. To me it seemed as if it brought me back to an old black-and-white movie, the effect was nostalgic. My dad stayed on the grind though, always finding ways to feed his family; he'd brought home some cans of food that was taken from a storefront that had caught on fire. The smell of smoked goods remained in my nostrils long after the food was gone.

Trouble in Paradise

My brother had begun to hang around with some guys on the street, this bothered my dad. He told my brother to stay away from those boys, but my brother didn't want to listen; he wanted to do what he wanted, and this became an issue. I don't know all what was said between them, but he went after my brother to kick his ass. My brother ran from him and jumped out of the second-floor window. When he did, he landed in the wrong position and broke his arm. My mother tried to stop him, but it was too late. Afterwards the ambulance was called, and the authorities got involved. When they arrived at the hospital, the police took a statement, and the case was referred to family court. It was a few days between the incident and the court appearance. When we did go, our whole family went before the judge.

All the children were dressed up in their Sunday best clothes and traveled to the courthouse. We had to take a train from our house to the city. On the way I remember the different train stations that appeared as we rode. We passed Canal St., The Bowery, Delancey and a few more stops until we got to City Hall (Center Street). The people spoke back and forth in a hush-hush fashion, everything was so serious, then we were all huddled into the judge's chamber. He asked us individually who we would like to stay with, our mother or father? We all wanted to stay with my mother. Then the judge ordered a decree that we should all stay with my mother back on Covert Street. We went back to the house and my dad was furious; he told my mother if she didn't take those kids and get the hell out of his house, he would burn it down with all of us in it. By the next week, we were back in our old house on Covert Street. I remember there was still turbulence going on even after we had left. I know my dad didn't want us to leave but it was probably better for all of us. In so doing he became angry and bitter; he took it out on us at times. He didn't pay the bills, or give us money for support, and the utility company finally shut off the water. We had to draw buckets of water for the house from a fire hydrant, which went on for a long while but that wasn't the end of it. He stopped paying the mortgage and the house went into foreclosure. We finally lost it and soon after had to move again. All my mother's hard-earned money that she sacrificed for just went down the drain because my dad didn't want to act right and communicate with her amicably. He would rather for us to lose the house to the bank than see my mother and her kids have anything. This must've hurt my mom something awful, but she never let on to us her angst or showed any anxiety.

My mom soon found an apartment down the street from the house we lived in on Covert St. It was on the second floor on top of a bike shop, right downstairs from my aunt Mary. There was an older white guy there who owned the shop, his name was Joe. I liked him as a person, but he was not too friendly. He didn't like people trying to get over on him, and he also had a mean German Shephard that barked if someone came too close. Sometimes Joe had to struggle to hold him back from biting people. Some days he would give me little things to do that helped him out, maybe put the spokes in a brand-new bike or change a flat tire, he would also send me to the store for him. I would buy him a coffee and a cruller donut, then he would tell me to keep the change.

I met my first girlfriend somewhere around this time; her name was Dolka, her family was from the Dominican Republic. She was so pretty with long black silky hair, smooth olive-colored skin, somewhat petite, and the most adorable smile. I can't remember what the circumstances were when we first met, but after the initial moments I spent most of my time with her. On the cool summer nights, we would sit on my stairs while it was dark outside my building just sitting and talking until, I walked her home. Her house was down the street from where I lived which made it convenient for us both. We also spent a lot of time French kissing when we could; hiding from the others was another issue we didn't want them to tease us. I wanted to have sex with her many times, but she wasn't ready and didn't let me; even tried to take her down in the basement of our building and still no deal. I was happy to kiss her and having her in my life. I woke up in the mornings feeling like I was so lucky, she made me feel special. We stayed together for a long time, maybe eight months until a guy from my class told me he fucked her. I was so infuriated that I beat her up which I regretted; then I tried to make up with her and get back together, but it was not the same. She told me that she didn't do it. I just didn't know what to believe. Then later one day, the guy who said she had sex with him was bothering her, so I beat him up also and told him to leave her alone. I spent many days in my house crying listening to Michael Jackson's "Be There." There were also other sad songs that came to mind; however, the thrill was gone.

My mom worked very hard trying to keep food on the table for all her children and as she did she became tired. She sometimes asked me to go to the laundromat for her. I didn't mind but she still offered to pay me to do it. It might be ten loads of clothes so I might have to make two or three trips. I would take the first load there and put it in the machines, then go back home to pick up the rest of them. For a kid only ten years old I was quite responsible. I was a great help to her at that age. She was always glad to have some help from us, as we were to give it. When I brought the clothes home, she and others would fold them up, while the rest may have had to go on the clothesline out the window, across the roof. In those days people stole one another's clothes if they could get away with it.

We stayed there for a while, and it became too crowded; it seemed as if I needed more space. At times, my brothers and I would fight for the dumbest things, and I got so tired of it. One day as my dad visited, we had a talk; I asked him if it was all right for me to come and live with him. I guess he was hurt and wounded from the separation, when he came by from time to time I was happy to see him. I can't say if my other siblings felt the same as I did, but he was still my dad. He looked at me and asked what's was going on. I told him what I was feeling, and he said, "Sure, you can come and stay with me. Now listen to me, what I tell you. You go and tell your mother what you want to do, and tomorrow you pack up all your belongings and when I come by, I'll pick you up and take you home with me." So that's what we did, the next day he came, and I left Bushwick Ave to stay with him.

There were a couple of rooms that were open, so he gave me one that he thought was good for me. I went in, felt a little strange being in a room all by myself but soon acclimated to my surroundings. At night my dad and I would talk over sharing snacks such as cheese and crackers, he shared many stories of his past, the things he went through from the time he was a child till the time that I knew him then. He was a short burly, dark-skinned man who would fight at the drop of a dime. People didn't really mess with him though, but I feel he was a fair man. I never saw him trying to take advantage of anyone. He always said he was a God-fearing man and he tried hard to live a good life. We didn't always have what we wanted, but we always seem to have what we needed.

He got up early in the mornings before work and put on breakfast for us. Most of the time we'd have some salt pork, eggs, and grits. He liked coffee with his, but I didn't care for it so much back then. He would make breakfast, then tell me what he wanted me to do around the house by the time he came back home. At first this was a problem for me because I would usually watch TV all day until he came back. If I hadn't done what he asked, he would have been upset. Many times, he talked to me about it, and it took a while before I could manage. I had to learn to do my chores first, before I watched the TV, because if I didn't, I wouldn't get anything done; I sure didn't like to make him upset. Things were fine when everybody played their part.

My dad fixed cars among many other things. It was a joy and a pleasure to learn from him. He would take his time to show me how to use certain tools, and also give me pointers about safety. I never thought about being a father and how to raise a child, but for him it was a process that I hoped gave him as much pleasure raising me as I did being raised. When you spend a lot of time with a person and you get to know them, they become a part of you, especially if they are of your blood.

It was nighttime, my dad had come home from work, and he was using the bathroom.

"Johnnie, I need you to go to the store for some toilet tissue." He cracked the door and handed me some money. "Go right to the corner store, get me some tissue and hurry back."

"Okay, I'll be right back." I put on my thin dungaree jacket my mother brought me, picked my afro, and locked the door. Outside the path was dark offset by the streetlight shining down on the Autumn leaves swirling up to a tempest on the sidewalk, they piled on top of each other in different hues cluttering the gutters. It might've been about thirty-five degrees that night, it was cold to me. There was hardly anyone else out, as I ran to the store. It was closed, so I journeyed to the next corner hoping to get back soon. It was a small inconvenience, but I got the tissue and started on my way home. While walking hurriedly on my way back, a medium height, brown skinned guy walked close to me and asked,

"You want to make some money?" I looked at him and said,

"Doing what?"

"Stamping the prices on some cans in a store."

Thinking of how poor and broke I was, or had been, not having nice clothes, girls looking down on me because I was poor, and this could have been my way out. I hated not having nice things and not being able to do for myself.

"I have to ask my dad first."

"Okay." We started walking, looking for a telephone booth. They had phone booths, or telephones on almost every corner back then. I reached in my pocket for a dime to call my house.

"Hello, dad it's me. I met this guy and he said he wants me to work in a store stamping the prices on some cans of food. Is it all right if I go?"

"No, you come right home now and forget that. I don't know anything about that person."

"Ah, Dad, it's okay, I'll be all right. I'll be home in a little while, okay."

"I don't think you should do it, but if you want to go then go."

"Okay, I'll be home in a little while. See you then."

Don't talk to Strangers

We walked for almost forty minutes, crossing Atlantic Ave. The Atlantic Towers was a newly built project, and we had just passed it. The wind was blowing hard as I clutched onto my little thin jacket. We arrived at Pacific Ave and Howard St. There were a couple of elder ladies and some kids playing in front of the building who the guy knew, they spoke to one another. We started walking up the dark stairs toward the top floor. When we arrived at the top I sat by the roof door on the stairs and that's when the guy positioned himself so I couldn't easily run past back by and get away from him and told me, "You are a fool." Right then and there every pore in my body seemed to open and an extreme fright went through my soul. My thoughts raced frantically but I didn't show it; I was near the roof, and I heard stories in the news about people who fell or were thrown off rooftops. My immediate reaction was to do whatever I had to do to survive. He started to show me pictures of him at his karate studio; back then it was a famous one called Jerome Mackey's, where he and another guy was sparring. It showed him jumping up in the air locking his legs around the other guy's neck and throwing him across the mat. I must have been intimidated, but I still wanted to be safe. No telling where this was going to end. I hope I wasn't that good-looking where these gay guys just shot out the woodwork hoping to get some action, either way, there was nothing in the world that I would have done to lead them to me, I only desired to be free from the presence of such a miscreant. I didn't realize that I had been so stupid as to have been led into an ambush, or something in similitude. This creepy miscreant wanted to pleasure himself by having me lay on top of him and kiss him with my pants on. I was so embarrassed and filled with angst, it was such a loathsome feeling that I didn't know what or how I should do. I wanted to whack him in his head and run, but I thought if I didn't finish him off in a quick motion I would have to be there, all alone fighting with this bastard whom I may, or may not overtake. So, I weighed my options and decided to wait for an opportunity to escape, after all, he was bigger than me.

So, after I laid on top of him and he came on himself he got up and told me he was going into an apartment below us to do something, probably went to wash off. Maybe he was going to get a knife to carve me up or any other creepy idea that may have come to his sordid brain. I just had to survive and get away. That was all I needed to hear; so, I slowly crept downwards onto the stairs behind him, with very little space between us, being as silent as I could, listening to every sound and every voice. He knocked on a door a couple of flights below where he left me as I waited in the lurch; someone came to the door, and he went inside. Grabbing the railings and sliding down the stairs as fast as I could not making any noise I made it to the outside door of the building and there was no longer anyone hanging around.

I started to go back home the way we came but decided he might go back that way if he came searching to find me. I ran in the opposite direction crisscrossing the streets and looking behind to make sure he wasn't following me. I walked and ran until I saw a familiar place; by this time, I was on the way to my mother's house, cold from the winds blowing and frightened; I rushed through the streets twisting and turning, checking behind me to see if I was being followed and finally, I made it. They were all there in a panic, and somehow they already knew I was missing from my father's house and asked me what happened. I didn't go into details, but the no-good foul children of the landlord started spreading the rumor that I was raped. Then began to taunt and tease me, pushing me to a very uncomfortable place. I was so embarrassed I wanted to lash out at them, but I was too troubled to mount a formidable defense. As I tried to get through the painful experience, it was just too unbearable; I returned to my father's house and became a recluse.

When my older brother came to New York from New Jersey, he would bring lots of his old comic books, with guns and car magazines. I spent much of my time reading them and avoiding people. Cooking and cleaning in the kitchen were a getaway, a relaxation. When I arrived back on the scene, I spent most of the day watching TV and sometimes doing other chores, but now I gained a liking to the kitchen work. I enjoyed washing the dishes while listening to the radio. There were so many artists who landed on my favorites list. I liked Barbara Streisand, Carly Simon, Bill Withers, Stevie Wonder, and many others. There I stayed in the kitchen all alone cooking food for my dad, washing the dishes, and listening to the latest music. I became oblivious to the things that went on in the streets, I stayed inside mostly tending to my hobbies. The bank had given my dad a trinket made of copper with replicas of coins on a tiny tree. He handed it off to me and I put it up. I also started a coin collection that had different kinds of coins and currency. I rolled nickels, pennies, and dimes, there were even a few stamps in there. One day I misplaced the money tree and couldn't stop looking for it; I walked up and down the street where we lived, in the gutters, by the sidewalks and just couldn't find it.

The days turned into months; as some of my siblings began to worry about me, I didn't do it intentionally, I thought it was the right thing to do, to stay away from everyone. I had lost my trust in people. This gave me peace. I no longer had an innocence that made me glow; instead, my aura was one with a lackluster appearance. I went through a spate of different emotions, all leading up to loneliness, melancholy, and depression. I was okay with being alone, just if I didn't have to face those evil, cantankerous children, who were anything except my friends. I thought about the times my mother asked me to go to the laundry to do our clothes, the nights when I was cold, and she would always manage to put a cover over me. How she was always there for me, and how much she loved me; I missed her, I was just far away and led a different life then.

I remembered most of my days before this incident happened, how I was a normal happy-go-lucky kid. The many days I walked around the neighborhood finding things to do, the stores and places I frequented, me staying with my aunt and uncle, having found, and courted my Dominican girlfriend, being taught how to French kiss. All the memories that I cherished and felt so attached to was now being eroded into a vague nothingness, replaced by the pervasive thoughts of that God-forsaken night.

A Mother's Love

Somewhere I heard it said that "There's no greater love in the world, than that for a mother towards her son." If this was so and my mother was concerned for my well-being, she decided to move the family and I to East Flatbush to remove me from the agony of being molested. At the time I didn't see it, or know it for sure, but that was how my mom was. She didn't always broadcast her intentions; she did things in silence. As she planned the move, I slowly decided to move back with her. The first apartment we lived in after Bushwick Ave was on Winthrop and East 91st. It was above a shoe storefront owned by a Jewish couple. At times the old man would try to talk to me, to school me. He said the guy who was in the apartment before us would also work for him. He stayed for many years working after school, until he managed to save up enough to buy a car. They asked me to help them out sometimes, which I didn't mind, it was a way to put a few dollars in my pocket. When we were getting the apartment ready, my brother and I would often go to White Castle to get hamburgers, fries, and fried clams. We'd be painting the walls of the apartment, drinking wine and smoking weed. My brothers were cool, and they always seemed to look out for me. I wished I hadn't picked up the cigarette smoking habit though but that is life, you win some and some you lose.

After living there for a while, I met the girl upstairs, a big-leg brown-skinned cutie pie named Teresa Kenon. She had a nice shape and a pleasant smile; I stayed trying to get to know her and she didn't seem to mind. We listened to her records while she talked to me about her life conquests, and her ambitions. It was such a joy to be with her, but I never really saw her as being my girlfriend. She was too fine, and she always told me that I was too young for her, I just didn't give it any thought. We gave her the name "the Wiggler," because when she walked her butt wiggled like nice thick jelly." I might go to her house and ask for her and her mom would look at me like, why is you entertaining that young boy. I was too inexperienced to move forward with my desires, but I was cool just being with her. She smoked Kool cigarettes, and I helped her not thinking of being a leech or a burden. I smoked Newport's, and I shared with her also when I had, so maybe I wasn't a real leech.

There was another girl named Barbara Perkins. She had a nice, thick round butt. I don't know why that was the first thing I looked at when I saw a girl, but it became like a Pavlovian response. I guess it's similar for dogs that sniff each other's asses when they meet. I tried to talk to Barbara many times and got nowhere, I felt like it was so unfair, because I really wanted some of her stuff. The thing was, I didn't know how to get a girl or to get laid. I hated wanting to have sex and no one to do it with me. I spent too many days masturbating, fantasizing about some girls that didn't want me or think about me the way I thought about them; that was a real pisser. As times changed, people changed, and my associations did too. I spent many of my days hanging out on the corners begging to get wine, beer or whatever, smoking cigarettes and chasing girls. When the guys and I reached our goal for the wine or beer, we would try to sing a song, probably a Doo-Wop. I can't imagine what a bad influence I had on the youth at the time. I never thought anyone looked up to me, I was just there.

People were always hanging around my family's house it seemed. They enjoyed my mother's hospitality and her good home cooking. At one time there was a whole family mooching off us, we called them "the Begga-boos." No matter what we had food-wise, if you offered, they hardly ever said no. Some people just don't have any dignity or self-respect; just because one of them was hungry doesn't mean a person should accept if you offer. I believe in letting a person eat in peace, especially if they don't have enough to feed you also. That subject can get weird at times. I remember a winter season outside by the Marcy projects, on the inside there was a group of young teens huddled around talking about passersby, when one came inside the hallway with a hero sandwich. Four, maybe five of them all wanted a bite from that one hero sandwich, and it was cool. Me myself I'd prefer to find a way to get my own. I couldn't stand around waiting for someone else to give me my sustenance.

The summertime eased in, and my cousin Cookie came from Philadelphia with her friend; a light-skinned girl named Natasha Galloway. She was about my age who was nice and easy to talk to. I spent a few happy hours getting to know her, keeping a close watch. When she walked through a door, I was there to open it for her; or if we needed something from the store we went together. We really hit it off immediately. It is something about beautiful young girls that always fascinated me. Before the night had turned back into day, I was in the bedroom with her trying to get me some. She let me so I pushed my cock in her belly, this was my first time doing it, and I was so amazed by the wonderful soft gooey feeling of her insides. I didn't perform right though because I didn't know what I was doing. I just pumped it up once or twice, maybe three times and regrettably got up off it. I think of it today and I feel so ashamed that I didn't give her the pleasure that we both were looking for, but she didn't complain. I felt like a lame for not knowing how to rock her boots. I considered my first-time having sex as a dud, a bigtime failure.

I had a snow-white Fuji 18 speed 27" bike that I rode frequently. It was a lifesaver when I wanted to go from one end of town to the other. I loved riding that bike, and it took me everywhere I needed to go. I had gone to my dad's house earlier that day and was on my way back home. I passed by Buffalo Ave somewhere around Saint Mary's Hospital when this young black dude yelled out to me, holding an object in a bag, "If you come by here again, I'm gonna take that bike." I kept riding slowly with my eye on him. I saw a cop car on the next corner and told them I wanted to check that dude, but I couldn't tell if he had a weapon in his bag, if they would come with me while I confronted him. They agreed and I rode back, "What you said before when I was riding by?"

"You heard me, I said I'm gonna take your bike."

"Okay, then do it." The police car rode up and checked him to make sure he didn't have anything in the bag. Then I got off my bike and said, "Do it." He came close and swung at me and I blocked his swing. He backed up then gave it another try, this time like a wild man. I blocked it again and then I put my hand up by his face, "If you swing at me one more time, I'm gonna bust your ass." He looked at me and decided that he didn't really want to do that, so I left, giving a thumbs up to the officers. They looked disappointed that I didn't kick the poor fool's butt.

The summertime was still nice though, in the mornings birds would sing all throughout the neighborhood while the sunrise took over the sky. We weren't doing too bad for a lower-class black family being raised by a single mother. Of course, if our journey with my dad had been more complete, then I think we all would have gone further in life. I was smoking cigarettes by the age of thirteen, doing weed and drinking alcohol as an early teen. It didn't really bother other people too much, but I did have my vices.

Sometime later my sister met a guy who was a jailbird and when he came out, he stayed with us. His name was Clarence, he was tall like me, light brown skinned with a pickled head, and he just didn't give a fuck. He was always in trouble using his jailhouse mentality; thinking he could bogart people and intimidate them. The best thing I liked about Clarence was he gave me weed; and he always spoke nice to me trying to elevate me with his Five-Percent knowledge. The Five-Percent Nation was supposed to be an offshoot of Islam, but it was clear that they were not a part of that religion.

On one warm summer night he copped a nickel bag of smoke and got eleven joints from it. He gave me one, I started smoking and sat back in a chair, looking around until suddenly, things began to appear kind of funny. Clarence crossed his legs and started speaking to me as if he was a gay person. I began to laugh uncontrollably, but I was high as a kite. Everything was looking funny now, the cars were moving slow, the people had a slurred speech, while other things seemed to be floating in the air, so after I had my fun, I went upstairs to my house and raided the refrigerator. I got my munch on then fell asleep, that was about all I did at that age; I wish my mindset was geared more towards an education and getting a career.

I often walked through the neighborhood looking for girls to talk to but didn't have much luck. Most of the girls were from the West Indies, and they didn't care to mix up with American black guys. It seemed like there was an unwritten law that giving American black guys rhythm was taboo. Many foreigners looked down on us as if they were better than. They always kept a condescending attitude when we interacted. White folk gave them better jobs, opportunities for housing, schools, and numerous of other things we didn't even know about. They hated us to a certain degree, so much so that we called each other racist names; they would call us "Nigger" and we might call them "Monkey." I believe we called every nationality slang names that was not a natural American. It was a bad habit we developed; it was even more bitter for us when we saw how the white man treated many others better and still looked down on us condescendingly. It seemed as if we were persecuted for not being able to kiss their asses and progress in this racist society, also to move forward and rise above our difficulties. These things we might have done if they didn't keep killing off our leaders such as Dr. King and Malcolm X.

I was now going to high school at George W. Wingate, and I didn't want to be there, I wanted to go to Brooklyn Tech, but the school officials in charge of placements said I didn't live in the right zip code, the (white) zip code. That was just another way they had of discriminating to keep me and others from going to that kind of school. My first year in Wingate I cut classes and spent most of my time playing handball. My friend Bump and I would get up early in the morning, get a forty oz. of beer and smoke a joint on the way to school. We always made sure that we went to our homeroom class at least, so we hopefully wouldn't get left behind.

It was such a bore going to that school at first, then I somehow managed to get into the medical science program for a while, thought maybe I'd get into medicine in some form. That didn't work, I left there and went into limbo until I found the co-op program. This program became my way out for a few good reasons, which was if I could live up to the criteria. I had to work a week and go to school for a week while maintaining an 80 percent average in my classes. It was going to be easy for me because I could do most of my schoolwork in my sleep if that was the only thing I had to worry about. I was happy to go to school now and meet new friends from the co-op program. It's kind of funny the difference a day makes, before I was self-conscious about my clothes and not having extra money for lunch, or other things. It was such a harsh reminder that I was a poor scruffy student with plenty on my plate. I came every day on time now and did my schoolwork then the supervisor of the program appeared to be proud of my achievements, I felt a sense of hope.

While I was in school, I heard that they were having a lottery for summer jobs for the youth, called the Youth Entitlement Program. The kids lined up two blocks long hoping to get a job for that summer. This was one of the most uplifting things a young person could hope for. I filled out the application praying that they would call me for this opportunity. That day I went home and hung around the neighborhood. Going to the park playing handball was one of my favorite pastimes, my brothers and I would get up early in the mornings during the summer months and play either handball or basketball. We would play vigorously sometimes smoking a joint in between games, drinking beer and hanging around the other people in the neighborhood. Some of them were gang-bangers that intimidated kids from the area, but not me. I guess I was too big for that crap, or they knew of my brothers who were known to be a terror. My brothers brutally beat several guys that interfered with our comradery. A few days had passed, and I got word that I was being hired for the summer job. I could have jumped out a 3rd floor window for all the joy of that moment, I was so happy. The postcard read that I should report to a supervisor named Mr. Roberts about a block away from my house on 91st Street. When that day came, I went and met Mr. Roberts where he had me fill out some papers then told me what he wanted all the participants to do. We were going to be painting and doing maintenance around the block. I usually arrived early and started working on that day's assignment. At first it was a little tedious, but after a while I looked forward to whatever he had in store for us. There were several other workers who seemed to enjoy that fact that we all had jobs. We figured out what we were going to spend our paychecks on before we even received them.

Being in the scorching hot sunlight would be unbearable at times, the people whose houses we worked on would often bring us water to help us quench our thirst. We drank the water and got right back to work; sometimes until it was time to knock-off and go home. As time went on the residents, who were mostly from the West Indies, offered us other side jobs for extra cash. It could have been painting their stairs, cleaning refuse from a backyard, lining up a fence, mostly small things that were not too difficult. There was an elderly lady who asked me to do side jobs for her; she was nice to me and that made me think of getting to know her. I thought about her having her own house and maybe getting more money for some of my good loving; but I didn't like the old lady clothes she wore, and the scent she carried, it was a stale funny smell. At that age my cock stayed hard as a brick and all pussy was subject to getting beat down; but it was however just a fleeting thought.

When lunchtime came, some of us might walk down the street and get a free lunch from one of the designated spots. They had bologna-and-cheese sandwiches, a fruit, juice, and milk. We might double up, and that solved the problem of hunger. Working so hard in that hot sun made me develop a voracious appetite. I could eat a couple of big plates of food regularly and wouldn't gain any weight. I did a lot of exercising back then.

Almost three weeks passed by as we signed for and received our first checks. I can't remember if I gave my mother any money at that time, but she most likely told me to spend it on myself. I could never buy all the things I wanted to, so I settled for what I could get. As a young teenager learning that your money doesn't go far is a valuable lesson. When you must provide for yourself, you can begin to see how hard it is for your parents to do for their children. I learned to appreciate my parents even more after I started working. The summer was ending now, and it was almost time to go back to school.

My Second Job

Before I left for the summer, I had expressed my desire to work in the co-op program and while I was working on my summer job, I was contacted by the co-op bureau concerning a position that might be available. It had been two months since I entered the program, and I was now going for my first interview the supervisor had set up for me. Even though I was not privy to the info, ins and outs of the meetings that were responsible for the change of heart in Corporate America's attitude toward hiring black school kids, it was a heaven send for me. These people could see the devastating effects their policies had on our communities by not giving us jobs, also how it placed our communities in turmoil. Fathers who were locked down in prisons away from their families, mothers raising numerous children depending on the welfare system, most of the entry-level jobs given to people of other nationalities. There was a list of things that went on and on about why things were the way they were. One thing I learned was it was hard to be involved in criminal activity if you are working hard trying to do the right thing. I can tell you plenty about the dynamics of our living conditions but, this is not a pity party.

Two days before I was to go to my first interview, I was given instructions on what to do when I go. Previously we spoke about many different things, such as what to wear, keeping eye contact, looking presentable, speaking from the heart appropriately and so on.

I left early that day and arrived on Wall Street about twenty minutes before 12:00 P.M. I asked someone if they knew where the address I showed them was located. They directed me to an area down by Water Street along the shore. I walked down and over and through some streets into a building, asking another passerby what time they had. They informed me that it was five minutes to 12:00 P.M. and I was panicking as I thought to myself, "how awful to be late on the very first chance to get a job." I remembered what I was told if I had any problems, to call the number I had on my papers. I put a coin in the telephone booth and let it ring, nervously.

"Hello"

"Hello, this is Johnnie Davis, I'm supposed to have an interview with you today at 12:00 P.M. but I'm lost."

"Where are you, Mr. Davis?"

"I'm at the Chase Bank by Water Street."

"Oh, I see, you are at the wrong Chase Bank, we are at One Chase Plaza, it's a little way off, you can come right up Wall Street to John Street, and you'll find us."

"Okay, I'll be right there."

I walked a few blocks and started sweating from the heat. There were people out in droves as food trucks cashed in on their vending products. I was a little hungry myself, but I didn't have time to even get a hot dog. I rushed into the building hoping that I still had a chance to secure this job. I hadn't really been around these kinds of folk and wasn't sure how to react or respond in a manner acceptable to them. I reached the thirty-eighth floor stepped out of the elevator and looked at the hallway leading to the firm. There were two huge glass doors that swung inwards to an immaculate waiting area. I approached the receptionist and told her who I was, that I had an appointment, then she handed me an application and asked me to fill it out. I filled it out and gave it back to her; she looked at it then told me to have a seat. I sat down for a moment looking at the breathtaking grand view of many areas of the city, near and far. While there a moment passed as Pat Cantone came out and spoke to the receptionist, she gesticulated towards me. Pat came over then extended her hand to me with a warm smile, "Hi, I'm Pat, Mr. Davis?"

"Yes, I'm sorry for being late, I was lost."

"Yeah, I know. Come with me." She took me to her office, and we spoke for a few minutes. She was a short lady, well dressed in business attire that represented the spirit of the firm; one who asked me about school, if I can handle it while working a week, going to school a week, I said "sure." Then she told me I would be making $2.67 an hour 35 hours a week. For somebody who was making $0.00 before that moment that sounded good to me.

"Let me introduce you to your new boss." We went up two flights and into a mailroom. There were newspapers, paper clips, postage machines, pens, tape and glue, everything needed to mail or ship a package was there and they all stopped for a second to greet me.

"So, you got lost, huh? Well, the city is big so try to pay attention to your surroundings."

"Yes, okay I will, I was trying to be on time, and I got lost." The boss's name was Melvin Mercer, an elderly white man, with short reddish balding hair with an air of determination. Melvin looked as if he came from my dad's era, through many of life's changing events of the century.

"You can start Monday and we look forward to having you aboard."

"Thank you, I'll be here then, have a nice day."

I was excited to tell my mom, as usual, she was happy for me; she wanted all her children to live a good life and be successful. For me, this was a great start by getting a job at a well-to-do law firm. That Monday I arrived early trying to find a spot on the bench to fit in with the crew; there were older gentlemen who seemed glued to their seats looking as if they didn't want to do anything. Most of them were retirees who were only working for some extra cash. The boss was happy to have me there to finally get some help with the volume of work being processed daily.

"Hey, Larry, show him how to operate the Pitney Bowes Postage machine."

Larry was from Africa; he'd been there for a few years now, knowing the average routine of a regular day. He showed me the basic procedure for wrapping, weighing, and stamping a package. Next on the list was getting the daily mail from the post office. There was a satellite post office a few blocks away from the firm which held the mail that had to be picked up every morning. The reason we didn't wait for them to deliver the mail was because half a day would have gone by if we waited on the post office to deliver. There was more than two hundred lawyers, partners, and associates, that were working in and out from our firm, Davis, Polk, and Wardwell. Imagine all the mail that was generated. I liked that we shared my last name which made me feel a little more significant. So, with all these people working there doing very important work, we couldn't afford to waste time in the period of the day needed to achieve our goals. The first thing was to retrieve the mail, then sort it into the pigeonholes at the office. Once all the mail was sorted and loaded on the carts, the pages would trek it to their respective offices. Sometimes the Lawyers would be in at that period in the morning, but mostly they hadn't arrived yet. The pages would just leave whatever they had for whoever. There were other departments inside the firm they had to deliver to also; we all made it work like a well-oiled machine.

After the morning mail was delivered there was time for a break, usually I'd eat at the cafeteria where the prices were cheaper than eating outside the building. Sometimes if I had time in the mornings, I would grab my breakfast at one of the greasy spoons with the best offers. Down by Wall Street there were a few cheaper deals for breakfast, in which I enjoyed bacon, eggs, home fries, toast, orange juice and coffee when I could. This was a good deal at some places where they had lowered the price to attract more customers. The sheer volume of customers was the factor that allowed them to stay in business and get paid. There were many rules to running a successful business, especially down in Wall St. Some were winners, and others lost by not being able to use a winning formula.

After getting breakfast and distributing the mail I would go to the uptown office located at 9 West 57th Street. The office space we used there was under the umbrella of the Morgan Guarantee Trust Company. This was one of the biggest banks on Wall St. **(Old Money)** which our firm had accounts with them, as with many other ones in that area. We were a huge cooperate law firm with offices in all parts of the world, New York; Washington, D.C.; Las Angeles, England; France; etc.

Once arriving at the mid-town office, I would find Warren, an older potbelly white guy and give him the shuttle bag. He would pigeonhole the mail and repeat the same process we did Downtown, distributing and delivering. I would then call my supervisor to inform him that I arrived; if there was anything that I needed to do while I was there, he would let me know. Many times, I had to make deliveries from that office, which was fine with me. I enjoyed walking and getting the tokens for carfare that I used to buy my lunch. All I had to do was take them to the token booth at any train station and cash them in. I could save enough for a hot dog, sausage, or a knish, which was all I needed to sustain me while I walked throughout Manhattan. Very rarely did I have to deliver in the other four boroughs.

Larry and I would often go to lunch together, he was a cool African brother, who hung out with me at lunchtime. We would pick up a pint of Bacardi Rum, some soda for a chaser, and a joint from one of the hustlers selling in the back-alley ways off from the main buildings. Larry also liked to play the OTB as did some of the other workers in the office. So, we would get high, play the horses, get some food, and go back to work. They gave us an hour for lunch, plenty of time to do all we liked. By the time I'd get back to work I would be flying. When the people looked at me, they could see by my chinchy eyes I was high and start to wonder about me. Hardly anyone said anything to my face, although I'm sure they wanted to. I usually tried not to be so obvious by holding my head a little low and by not engaging in their conversations, also by just passing their offices. This went on for a long while until my new supervisor, Ramon Rosa, spoke to me about it. He told me he didn't mind what I did when I was off the clock or at home, but when I was working for him, he didn't want to see me high. I accepted his demand by not doing that as he suggested and staying focused; after all, he was right.

The next week I was back to school and the comradery of my friends in the program. Many of us had gotten jobs through the program and this made a difference in our lives. There was a place not far from the school that made the best hero sandwiches, which I liked a lot, and it was only a few blocks away. Having enough to afford lunch now made a big change in the way I felt about going to school. I became more responsible and began to study harder trying to understand the material so I could graduate on time.

While I tried to focus on my studies in my class, in from nowhere came this beautiful, lovely girl, who was nice, tall with creamy light brown skin and the whitest teeth I had ever seen. When I first met her, I was mesmerized, struck by her beauty. I wanted to talk to her and find out my chances for a love connection, I just didn't know how to go about it, guess I was sort of bashful too. One of the things I did was to brush my teeth with peroxide and baking soda a few times a week until there was a noticeable difference. So, when I was in that class trying to engage in my work, she would come by me or pass by, and I would lose my concentration. If I looked into her eyes, I became lost; they seemed to sparkle which set me ablaze, and she spoke so soft and clear as if she wanted me to indulge her in conversation. Her clothes were fancy, made exclusively with class. I surely didn't want to be deluded and edify something that was not there. Many times, I was rejected in the past trying to cross that bridge, relationships were hard to conceive for me as I never could make the right moves, no matter how hard I tried.

Anyway, I avoided her as much as I could but there was something about her presence that was so compelling. Her name was Debra Nash; this made me think of Johnny Cash the country singer, could she possibly be of some relation to him I thought in a fleeting moment, then following up to the thought, her ancestry was from Haiti. There were other girls in the school that thought of me in a special way, I just wasn't on my best lover-boy game. As the weeks ended, I often thought about Debra, if she might like to go out with me to be my girlfriend or if any nice cutie pie would for that matter. When I'd get home all those thoughts didn't seem to matter anymore, being back in my neighborhood made me feel as if I was transformed into another world. I really thought our scenery was very special, from the nice, beautiful trees, to the well-built brick houses that lined most every block for miles. There was a difference in the ascetics of the foreign cultures. The people that lived there were from numerous nationalities of the Caribbean Island, which previously belonged to the Jewish people who had sold much of their property to get away from black folk. Looking back at the past, I understand more why things were that way. Nobody wanted the blacks to be around them because of the misery and grief that black folk brought with them. Many of them were uneducated with little or no moral values, also not having had too much if any guidance. At times racial tensions did flair up but nothing too serious ever came from our confrontations. It was mostly name-calling and jealousy that spawn our reactions. As Afro-Americans, we had to endure many West Indians coming to this country getting better jobs, housing, and other opportunities thrust into their laps, being granted full access to our resources, while Afro-Americans had to eat the scraps of this society that we had done so much to build. No matter what major contributions were made to this nation, there was very little recognition in the end. We were looked down on condescendingly, also ostracized in most places we worked in, last hired and the first fired.

I usually woke up about 5:30 A.M.; my mom would have my pants ironed. I'd jump in the shower, get dried off, dressed, then sat for a moment to a cup of tea with a slice of freshly squeezed lemon with five sugars, I liked it sweet. Then I thanked my mom and headed out the door. There would be a dollar cab that came down my block each morning picking up his regular fares for the Utica Ave train station. I'd get on the train about at 6:15 to 6:30 A.M. and arrive at Wall St. before 7:00 A.M. There was no punch clock, so I only had to have the boss acknowledge me. When I got there, he might tell me to go with Larry and get the mail at the auxiliary mail station, then come back and sort it out. So after that, I went to the uptown office by taking the 4 or 5 train that traveled on the Lexington Ave line. Then I reached the mid-town office carrying the checks, petty cash, and other packages. I'd sit for a few minutes before I had to make my way back. It would sometimes be as hot as the Dickens outside and I might be drenched with sweat under my clothes. The heat was sweltering above ground and throughout the subway system; the hot humid air pushed slowly through the platforms while the passengers sort relief by moving closer to the tunnel's entrances, the air that was forced through the tunnels was sporadic, but very soothing.

The train came to the 59th Street station and I boarded; it was the Lexington Ave Express going to Atlantic Ave. I entered the back end and started moving toward the front. As I passed through, I came to one car and spotted an extremely beautiful light-skinned girl sitting next to a guy who looked as if they were together. I sat down across from them surreptitiously watching them, waiting to see if they interacted. My hormones slowly skyrocketed through the roof; I wanted to talk to her so bad I could have jumped out of my skin. In my mind, I thought "what would I say to her?" She was drop-dead gorgeous, and I could see the more I surveyed her; my mind filled with lines I could say to her, while the guy she sat next to said absolutely nothing. Then I thought to myself, if they were together, why weren't they speaking to one another? There must have been thousands of girls I tried to talk to before her, each one striking out in succession. How I hated wanting a female in my life and not having one, at least one that wanted me as much as she. My stop was getting closer, and I figured if I didn't say something soon my opportunity to meet her would be lost like the countless ones that got away. When the train stopped and the guy she was sitting next to left; then I got up from my seat and moved next to her, looked her deep in her eyes and said,

"Hello, may I ask you a question?"

Looking kind of puzzled she said, "Sure."

"Are you a model?"

"Yes, I am, I do sometimes."

"My name is Johnnie; I didn't mean to stare, but I really wanted to meet you."

"Okay," she said smiling, "my name is Stacy."

"Stacy, what?"

"Stacy Stanislaus."

"Would it be alright for me to get your number and call you up sometimes?"

"I'm afraid I can't right now, I just moved to where I'm at and we didn't get the phone on yet."

"Would it be alright then to write you a letter?"

"Sure, I guess so." I had already passed my station (Wall St.) to get back to my job, but I was determined to make this connection happen. Her clothes were clean pressed as if they were brand new, her hair was shiny and black laid down into a ponytail, like she had just come from a professional hairdresser. When she smiled her teeth were so white and clean, I was astonished. I took out a piece of paper and asked her to put her address on the paper. She told me something and I handed her the paper for her to write it down. She wrote it down and I said to her,

"If this is not the right address, I will come out there and I'll find you." Re-membering so many others who liked to play games, I had to throw that in there. She smiled back at me keeping eye contact as she slowly moved out of my sight, then another female I knew appeared as I started to navigate my way back to the job. She was my friend's girlfriend looking like she wanted me to give her some rhythm too. I don't want to blow my own horn so I'm not going to, I'll just say I think I looked good enough for some of the ladies to want me.

When I got back to the job the first thing I did was ask the boss for a pen and paper to write the letter. I started to write and didn't finish until I had about 5 maybe 6 pages then I sealed it up, placed it in an envelope and mailed it off. I was so happy and jubilant thinking I had found someone to be with. Some of the workers questioned me about what I was doing. They felt good for me even though it might have been a bit unlikely.

The hours turned into days, while days passed for me waiting for a response to my letter. At that time, I was starting to get more recognition from girls, some from the neighborhood, others from different places. I was on a quest to get laid and fill my pockets with some cash. I bought DJ equipment and played my music at different places. I got better the more I practiced expanding my popularity. People asked me, "Are you JD, the guy who be playing music out the window, on Clarkson Ave, I think I know you." Some of the people I saw did know me, or of me; not that I was looking for fame, but it came with the territory especially for many of those who made it in the industry. I had come a long way from the days I first started out in school, I was able to buy things for myself and others if I chose to. I didn't really mind sharing with my friends and splurging on beer and weed when I came home from work. After a while it became a useless bore getting high every day. Sometimes I just wanted to chill out and enjoy a regular day without being bent, a moment in time that I could actually remember.

While walking around with my homeboy Irving, Teresa's brother, I met this young girl who was hanging out of her window a couple of blocks from my house. As I walked by her place, I spoke up to her through an opened window,

"Hey baby, what's going on?" She looked down to me and said,

"Hey guy, how are you doing?"

"I'm fine, but I could be doing better if I was with you." She looked at me and spoke.

"Is that so?"

"Yeah, I would." At that moment, another young boy started passing by saying,

"Hey man, what are you doing talking to my woman?" I looked at him like he was joking,

"That's your woman? You sure?" To myself saying "If that's your woman, then why is she talking to me."

"Okay." I kept on walking up the block, not wanting to make a scene.

The next day or two I passed the same block, and she was hanging out her window again.

"Aye gal, what you are doing up there?"

"Nothing much, waiting on you I guess."

"You want to drink some beer with me?"

"Okay, that's nice."

I went to the store quickly and bought two 40 oz. of Colt 45 and some weed. Then I handed it to her and asked her to roll it up. We sat around chit-chatting for a little while as I looked over the place. It was a nice small apartment with not too many amenities, but it was decent. The young lady's name was Star, I think. She lived there with her sister who had two children which Star was babysitting. They were kind of small, still using bottles and in diapers. After Star and I smoked the weed and drank most of the beer, she called me in the next room. She came close to me looking in my brown eyes with the look as if I done fucked up now. Grabbing me around my neck, she started kissing me telling me I could get it. I took my cock in my hand for a second, then got close on it and tried to ram it deep in her belly, but it wasn't that simple. She was kind of tight and had developed muscle control so as I pushed it in her pussy, the pussy grabbed my dick as if they were hands and squeezed it hard. I said to myself, "Ooohhh Boyyyy." That was the best stuff I ever had to this day. I pushed it in some more until I felt the back wall of her belly. I stayed in her pumping it for a few minutes then ejaculated in her; there was no real after-play, just a thanks and "I'll see you later." I went down the stairs and thought to myself that was the Bing, Bing, Bomb.

The days of summer were still warm, work had gotten much better thanks to another co-worker who showed me how to access more money on my out-of-town trips. It was all a matter of getting receipts for the services I was entitled to and turning them into the office for reimbursement. The firm had switched bosses from Mr. Mercer to a very wonderful Italian guy by the name of Mario Pino. Mario was by far one of the best people I've ever met in life. He always looked out for me even though he sometimes caught flack behind it; guess he just took a liking to me, as I did him. One of the reasons I guess he liked me is because I was a hard worker. From the moment I arrived in the morning, I was a great help in the office, and this made his life easier. He shared his life experiences with me, and I found them fascinating. He told me he had married a nun. I don't know how that was possible, but I accepted it. The other older gentlemen at the job were angry because I was being given many of the out-of-town trips which they felt more entitled to. It hadn't occurred to me that it would be a problem. This was because I was a young black student working twice as fast as some of them, they would even try to hide from work whenever they had the opportunity. Mario was also trying to hook me up with one of the girls there too. I remember there was this one white girl who was one of the secretaries' sister. I had it hot for her because she was a pretty, thick, big-leg, white girl with these pretty green eyes, or grey or whatever they were, I only knew she was awesome.

Almost every day on my way home, the folks in my neighborhood would be out mulling around enjoying the day. Some of the girls must've liked me too, by the way they said my name. "Hi Johnnnnieeee," with an extended nnnn-eeee on the end, this made me look at them inquisitively. "Why she says my name like that?"

"Hey gal, I might say."

It took some time to figure out, but eventually I did. She wanted to get next to me I thought. I must have been a bit obtuse not thinking so much about it. So, one day as I was riding my bike Carol asked me for a ride, I told her I would ride her, so she got on. We first rode a few blocks away and I bought a forty oz. of beer. We both drank from the bottle before I rode on. When we finished I decided to ride towards Prospect Park. That was kind of far I guess, but I was stronger then. When we reached there I had to take a leak. Then she did also, so she went into the bushes and pulled her pants down. I had my back turned for a moment, then I peeped at her, I couldn't resist. She had a nice fat bush, and I liked what I saw. When she returned from the bushes I took her up in my arms and started fingering her pussy through her pants. She said "stop, don't do that." I don't think she really meant it by the way she sounded. It was more like "oh that feels good." Then we started doing it in the park where I didn't see anybody but us there. It lasted maybe less than five minutes. Then I rode her home back on the bike. I didn't know if she was sore when I got her home, but I was surprised to have had sex with her. I liked her as a friend, but I thought she was too young for me. I was Seventeen and she said she was fifteen, but it seemed like she knew more than me. I was still afraid of going to jail and I didn't think about a relationship.

On some days I rode out to Flatbush from where I lived to find out if I could see the girl I met on the train who said her name was Stacey. I was so disturbed about not being able to get with her since our chance meeting. I really wanted to see her again, to make something happen if it could and bring my best to her. Every chance I got I rode out there on my bike to the address she gave me and hoped I would see her again. The first day I rode out there, I was in the general area and thought to myself it might be a while, so I decided to get some beer to help past the time. I rode down to a side street next to Ocean Ave till I came to a store that looked a little out of date. There were some people in there of a Latin descent, the shelves were stocked minimally, looking as if they were going out of business, and it reeked with the smell of cat urine. I was in a hurry to get back to the building where I was going to post up. The address was a huge apartment building with a doorman that was observant of me drinking beer on the perimeter. I quickly guzzled three of the 16 oz. of Budweiser, then I just sat and waited for people to pass by. After a few minutes sitting on a low brick wall, I began to feel a little tipsy. I kept watching to see if I saw her. Then after almost two hours there, a guy and a girl walked out of the building from across the street; they were together, but I couldn't tell what he was to her. I was across the street, and I could see that it was a possibility that she was the girl I was looking for. I knew I had to be wise not to screw it up; that could have been her father she was walking with, or her boyfriend or her brother. I had to wait for her to be alone to approach her. So, I waited on the wall while I was almost finished my six-pack; she came out the building again with other people and they piled into a Cadillac and took off. I was wondering if I should stay or leave. I decided to leave, happy that I at least saw someone who looked like her and that it was even possible that it might be her. The sky was ready to get dark, so I started to pedal home almost 4 miles away, and it was worth it. By the time I got home, I was so tired. I fell asleep and didn't wake up till the next morning.

I was back in school this week. The teacher had planned a little party sort of, she could see how much I liked Debra; thinking I was too shy to ask her out; she had planned to try and get us together. The whole school sort of knew about us by now, they knew how much I liked Debra, but she wasn't feeling me like that. The teacher played music that had very sentimental meanings to me and Debra. *After the love is gone, by Earth Wind and Fire, Still by Lionel Richie, Too Hot by Kool, and the Gang.* After listening to the music, I was moved to do something, just didn't know if there was anything I could have done to change our outcome. I knew in my mind the songs she was playing would stick in my head for many years to come, one reason was these were some of my favorites in my collection. It was as plain as day that Debra didn't want to be involved with me because I was a Black

American. This was a prevalent attitude throughout the city then. It was weird for me trying to get some love from most every girl I thought was good looking or sexy, and most of these types were from the West Indies. When class was out, I tried to follow Debra to talk to her. A few blocks away from the school I thought she saw who I was, and I stopped in my tracks so embarrassed that she might have saw me, I sort of hid behind a tree or something not knowing what to say. Why was this world like this? I was only a young guy trying to find happiness with a nice young girl; it was just too much to bear.

The school year was going to end soon, and I was not in good academic standing concerning my attendance. I had missed too many days to get a diploma, my supervisor told me. He said "If you go to night school and pass the GED, he'll change the GED for a regular diploma. So, I went to Washington Irving High School at night for four maybe six weeks.

It was sort of tough for me; I either had to go to school all that day or work and then go to night school. When I took my break for dinner, I would go in this deli I found; they had smoked Whitefish, or Chubb I forget the name, but I had that with maybe a bagel and a pickle or something similar. After a few weeks of showing up and doing the work, I passed the test. When I told my supervisor, he said he could not change it for me like he told me he would. Another disappointment to add to my hard-working young life. I did manage to get my GED though, even if I wasn't able to exchange it. The supervisor, Mr. Ginsberg, reneged on his offer. I never thought about all the things I was doing in my early life, how so many others in my category didn't do half as much as I; not to blow my own horn but I was dynamic. There was also an auxiliary military recruiting office on the school campus. I thought about going into the Air Force; I even took a battery of test to get in, while they kept making excuses not to let me in. You would never think the US armed forces would discriminate against me because they didn't want black folk in that branch of service. For whatever reason after going through all the steps and the tree didn't bear fruit; I just gave up on that dream, I became discouraged. I was planning on going into the ROTC program, this would have made me an officer after completing training. They asked me to get my medical records from when I was a five-year-old from Kings County Hospital when I had fell ill with problems to my kidneys, and that was the end of it for me. I had passed all the tests, made every appointment and they just kept adding shit on, I couldn't take any more delays or postponements.

It was hot and barely tolerable this beautiful summer day; I had come from work and decided to ride out to Flatbush again to find the girl who was the object of my adoration. I thought I must try hard to find out if the girl I saw was her. She might move soon, or maybe find somebody if she didn't have someone already, I just needed answers. I brought the unopened letter I initially wrote her and a mixed cassette tape of me DJ-ing music. I got on my Fuji and road out there again. When I arrived, I went to a building across from the address she gave me; I went inside and spoke to the doorman. I explained to him what I was doing there. He looked at me and said, "Those kids outside might know her, she could be one of those people from the TV show." I didn't think about what he said, I just hoped that they might know her. I slowly walked up to the children and asked one of them if they might know the girl I was looking for. The first one was a little leery and didn't want to talk to me because I was a stranger, I guess. Then the next was more receptive and told me,

"I think you are talking about my sister; her name is Debbie, and she will be coming from school at any moment now from that direction." I walked towards the corner waiting patiently, looking in the general vicinity from where she should be coming. The sunlight began to twinkle and glitter with extreme brightness, there she came walking down the street with the air of a royal blooded person. As she came closer, I gave her the once over, looking like a million everything was immaculate and right in place. She had on a pair of pure white cotton jeans moving towards me with her hair set in a ponytail. Her blouse was a soft pastel color, well made in some designer fashion.

"Excuse me, is your name Stacy? my name is Johnnie, I met you a long time ago on a train coming from Manhattan and we spoke."

Looking a bit surprised she said, "Sometimes people call me that, so you spent some time looking for me, huh?"

"Yes I told you if you gave me the wrong address, I would find you; I've been coming out here for almost a year hoping to see you again. I'm so glad. To finally meet you again. From the day I met you I had a fire burning in my heart for you." She smiled as I gave her the mixed tape and the letter marked "Return to Sender."

Well, I just came here to give you these things and was hoping if you will let me call you up sometime, did you get your phone in yet?"

"Yeah, I did." Reaching into her bookbag for some paper and a pen she wrote the phone number down. I put it securely in my pocket and asked her if it would be all right to call her later that night.

"Sure, that would be fine." If I died at that moment and went to Heaven, I was never so happy as I was then in my entire life. High on the clouds elevated as the sounds of joy and happiness filled the air. I reached down for my bike gave her a hug and reluctantly left. I wished that I could have stayed with her all that afternoon. Riding back home I looked at the people on the streets, they seemed to be wrapped in their respective worlds; mostly contented with the surety of living in a pleasant community. I passed through many neighborhoods on the way home, some were more downtrodden than others. As it stood, Debbie lived in an exclusive neighborhood, which was kept up by the well to do. There was hardly any litter on the streets or people hanging out on corners drinking and carrying on.

I reached home happy and elated, barely able to wait for the moment I could hear Debbie's voice on the phone. It must have been about 6:30 or 7:00 P.M. when I dialed her number. The phone rang for a few times then someone answered,

"Hello."

"Yes, hello."

"This is Johnnie, may I speak to Debbie please."

"Okay, hold on a minute." The person went to get Debbie and there was a little teasing in the background. "Stop playing, give me the phone." She handed the phone to her,

"Yes, hello."

"Hello Deb, this is Johnnie, how is it going?"

"Pretty good and you?"

"It is going great, now that I finally got a chance to meet you again."

"I think I would have died if I didn't see you one more time."

"Really, wow. That's special."

"Yeah Deb; I've been riding out by you for almost a year, I guess. I didn't know if you were the girl I was looking for or if you might move before I found out. I was so torn that I had to take a chance and hopefully it was you."

"Do you think you might have some free time soon that I can spend with you?"

"I don't know right now; I'll have to see."

"That will be great, I'm free anytime you have available."

"Okay, I'll let you know."

"All right then, let me let you go for now, have a good night."

"Okay Johnnie I will, you are too."

We both hung up the phone. In that instant I was filled with jubilation, my senses were overwhelmed, and the patter of my heartbeat seemed like loud drums. I thought to myself how lucky I was, and how desperate I was not to lose this chance for love. There had been many times when it just slipped through my hands; but this could not be one of them if I could help it. I spent so many years trying to find the right girl to be with, the random encounters meeting them on the streets, in office buildings, by the bus stations, on the train platforms; getting their numbers only to find it wasn't the correct information. Yes, it had been a long arduous journey searching to find that special someone.

The morning came slowly as the sun rose in my window; the birds were singing their usual melody for the sunrise it always seemed like a grand entrance to the skies. Mom was up already making breakfast for me, I washed quickly and headed for the city. As I went down into the subway, I bought a few tokens to travel with, collected my change and walked downstairs to the lower platform. The station was really crowded this time in the morning, so I had to be prepared to stand up when the train arrived. The 2, and 5 ran on the platforms which were very fast getting to the city. It might have taken about 30 minutes and ran like clockwork every day. Being dependable it was hard to screw up if you develop a routine. The same people you see road the trains most of the time, no matter where you are in the city. Those who were firmly attached to the workforce paved the way for the rest of the economy to grow. Being in the Wall St. area at lunchtime was an exciting experience. There were vendors selling all kinds of things as well as food carts. When I first started working and didn't have a budget to eat a proper meal, I would hope the boss gave me enough fares to cash in my carfares to get a couple of franks, hot sausage, or a knish. After settling in in my later years on the job, I might go for the pizza specials, overstuffed sandwiches, or gyros. They all helped me to appreciate my position as a messenger. I had access to most of the city and the best meals it had to offer, I was always looking for a new place to grab a meal. If I ate at a place and the food or the service was bad, I didn't usually go back. My day went fine, and I made it home, settled in and made a call to Debbie.

"Hello, Debbie?"

"No one second." She passed the phone to Debbie and gave us some privacy.

"Hello."

"Yeah, this is Johnnie."

"I know, how are you doing?"

"Pretty good, thanks."

"Just got off work a while ago."

"Okay, I was thinking if you are not busy this weekend, would you come over for a baby christening and meet my family?"

"Sure, that would be great. What time is it going to be?"

"About 11:00 A.M. on Sunday."

"Okay, I'll come. Should I bring anything?"

"No, just you." When she said that, I felt special, bringing a smile to my face.

When Sunday came, I went to Pitkin Ave that morning to buy a shirt to wear at the get together. I had some nice clothes; but not for the occasion, I wanted to look especially nice to impress her. Back then the stylish clothes were made of Gaberdine, a polyester material, so I looked at the knit shirts they had available. I must have paid about $20 or so after looking over the entire inventory. The shirt had a light grey, black, and green pattern which was okay for me. I went home took a shower and put on the shirt and noticed it had a flaw in the stitching. The shirt was an imperfect copy that the store sold me in my hurry. At first, I felt awful because I wanted to look nice but now, I had to decide whether I should wear the new shirt and get there as fast as I could or try to wear something from the mediocre clothes I already had. I decided to wear the imperfect one, even if it had a flaw.

I arrived a bit early not knowing what to expect hoping to make a good impression. I rang the buzzer and waited for an answer. Somebody buzzed me in, and I went to the elevator and rode to the floor. As I went in everyone was happy that I made it, showing their gracious hospitality. Debbie was still getting dressed so I waited for her to appear; in the meantime, her baby sister entertained me with some knock-knock jokes. Finally, Debbie came out wearing a purple pleated dress with her pretty hair combed back into a ponytail again. Her teeth were still as white as snow on a cloud of cotton. She had a gleam in her eyes emanating from her soul, a joy, a happiness waiting to be discovered, waiting for me. She came closer,

"You look nice, Johnnie; did you have any problems getting here?"

I was without my bike and my new shirt was sagging a little.

"No, I took a cab here.

"That's fine, did it cost a lot?"

"No, not too much?"

"Well, we are getting ready to go to the church. You come with me."

"All right."

We left the apartment building and went to a Catholic Church right on the next block. There were plants and flowers outside with a statue of Jesus holding his hand out to us. Debbie led me in and showed me where to sit. I sat behind a small group of people waiting for the ceremony to begin, looking around trying to take it all in. Suddenly, the person in the row in front of me turned her head around, and it was Thelma from *Good Times*, the smash hit sitcom show of that period. Everybody loved her, and she was that big TV star and then she spoke

"Hello, I'm Bernadette." I looked at her and I almost jumped out of my skin, I tried not to show how surprised I was, but I was in complete awe. I had no idea that she and Debbie were sisters. I didn't want to let on that I knew of her, also not wanting to seem uncouth. We all stood up and proceeded to engage the baptism. It was one of the most wonderful moments I had ever experienced, I didn't know what to say or do but they were all so gracious, allowing me to be a part of their faithful experience. We finished up there and took a cab to Brownsville. They had family there, and the whole entourage headed for it. We arrived and they played music on a record player console, offered me a beer, which I turned down, and they fed me well. The food was so delicious, and the company was out-standing. When we left, I wanted to kiss Debbie, but I was too shy and nervous. I guess she figured it out even though I never did. It was hard growing up as a teenager in those times, especially trying to navigate through finding and securing love. I wished I had more experience, but I only had a small number of incidents of interacting with girls, this made me some type of mindless dote.

The next time I spoke to her, Debbie asked me to come over for her baby sister's birthday party. Her little sister was a beautiful, lovely girl, who looked up to Debbie and did whatever she told her to. I really liked their whole family, and her mother was especially nice to me. Her father Greg was a slim medium sized guy that dressed very well like a player. He told me that he owned a liquor store on Flatbush Ave. which wasn't too far from their apartment. His hair was trimmed to a tee, not a thing out of place, you can tell he took a lot of pride in his appearance. Also, she had two older brothers: one was named Trel if I remember correctly, and the other one I forgot his name. I saw them both as caring, loving, and protective. One of them was graduating from Brooklyn College with a law degree, and lastly they had a dog whose name was Sergeant—Sarge for short. Anyway, when I arrived, Debbie had another fella who was also there to win her affection. I had competition and I was kind of jealous and upset for having to compete for her. I felt like this is bullshit. I think they offered me some beer again, and I turned them down on that note, then I decided to go out and try to find a birthday card for her little sister. Wouldn't you know it when I went out the friend from one of the buildings I delivered to was in the same neighborhood walking about. We were speaking and just then as I was talking to her, I guess Debbie, who felt that I was upset came looking for me to try to fix it. She saw me with my friend the beautiful young lady that was very attractive and may have gotten the wrong impression. Me and Debbie went back to the party, and I explained to her what I was doing, how I went out to get a birthday card and that's when I saw my friend. Later that day one of her brothers who had heard the mixed tape of my music, asked me if I wouldn't mind playing at Debbie's Sweet Sixteen coming up. I was flattered and told him yes of course. We spoke a little more about it then I went home. There were some other guys that rapped for me as I DJ. I had to let them know ahead of time so they would be available to help me there and back on that night. I told Debbie's father I had a few people that were going to help me, and he needed to know the exact number so he could inform the caterer. I kept the number to the minimum people that played with me all the time while we practiced, but I had a dilemma. My friend Irving didn't take good care of his teeth, he had the yuk mouth, and he was a bit off. I don't like to talk condescending about people, and I don't try to act like I'm better than; I just knew that if I let Irving come with us, he might give our crew a bad impression, I couldn't help it if he had the Yuk mouth.

When the day came and we arrived there that night, all of Debbie's good friends were there in the latest fashions looking like fine little movie stars. I had not told my friends who we were going to play for, but I felt it shouldn't matter. They, Debbie's friends, were dressed in the best clothes and hairstyles. They were all so lovely and gifted, floating around having fun, talking to each other and edifying Debbie's glorious day, Bernadette was there with her boyfriend, some guy from the West Coast and everybody was having a super great time. Me and my partner Bumpy played all the latest records while her friends went crazy on the dancefloor, they were expert guest. I played the record "Good Times" by CHIC over and over, not because her sister played Thelma in that show (*Good Times*); it was because that song was the number one song on the record charts, at that time for many weeks. I remember someone had a newspaper replica saying, "*Overnight Sensation,*" which was a hit by *Jerry* . Other hits as well were "*I'm Ready*" by *Kano*, "*Take your Time Do it Right*" by the SOS Band, "*Bounce Rock Skate*" by *Vaughan Mason* and many others. Greg also asked me to play some Rockers or Reggae music if I had any, he was a little upset because he wanted to represent his culture. The family was West Indian, I guess, but many of us thought they were African Americans. It didn't really matter to me just as long as I could keep talking to Debbie. At one point I broke in with the song from *Dennis Brown*, "*Bubbling Love*" and "*How Could I Leave.*" When I played those songs, Greg calmed down.

It was all a coincidence, but I felt like I landed on top of the world, sitting on a big fat lovely cloud. Debbie's dad Greg asked me to slow the music down so Debbie could have a slow dance with her other guy. I think he was undermining me and Debbie trying to guide her towards the competition. When I played the slow jam, her friend grabbed her arm and started putting his moves on her. Somehow, I managed to mess up the song by interrupting the music and they didn't get a chance to finish their dance. I can't say if I did that on purpose, maybe it was subliminal or if it was just a mistake, but I was happy I did. Soon after Debbie cut the birthday cake and gave me the first and biggest piece, I was so flattered. It was filled with so much cream filling and a few toppings, and the food was out of this world. Everything was so memorable and wonderful; I never regretted a moment since the day we met. She made my life jubilant, roaring with passion like a fairytale that had come true. After all the things I had been through in my life she made up for a lot of the tragic wrongs I'd endured, also she had a firm grasp on my heart.

While delivering packages on the Upper West Side, I was crossing the street, right in the middle as I walked, I got an extreme urge to scratch my balls. This happened more than once so at first, I didn't know what to think of it. Later that day when I reached home, I took a good look down on my body; I saw a little bug stuck to my skin. I tried to pull it off, but it just held on tighter, until I got a tweezer. I finally got it off, examined it and asked my brother what the hell this critter might be? He explained to me that I had crabs. I had only been with that other girl most recently, and she must have given it to me. He told me that I should see a doctor, so that's what I did when it was all over, I had to get a special shampoo and wash the infected area a couple of times to kill all the crabs and their eggs. I was glad to know that I would be okay, but I had to tell the young lady about my situation. I went over and told her, but she acted like it was no big deal. I just left swearing that I wouldn't be seeing her again, even though she had the best stuff I ever had.

I went home and thought about what I was going to tell Debbie. I couldn't face her with this story; she would never want to see me again. It's not like we were older and been through a lot in life. Things were just so wish-washy. I remember leaving my house, going to this Haitian restaurant two doors down from me to use their phone. I couldn't afford anyone ease dropping on my conversation. So, before I got there, I drank a few beers and I started talking to Debbie, I remember telling her about some of the events in my past, when that stranger molested me, when I saw that alien creature when I was small and when they took my footprints as a brand-new child. This must have seemed too incredulous for her to accept, while I was delivering these events to her, I failed to mention that I had come to tears; the memories of my past were so overwhelming to share. She was still a teenager, probably with more pressing issues than to console me. This was probably a mirror of my future with her; the weight of the moment could have had no greater impact on my future. This was the moment that she was to abandon me, the instant she gave me my walking papers right there on the spot; she didn't say it, but she didn't want to be bothered anymore for numerous reasons, but her other guy might have been another cause, how devastated I was. The thing I tried not to do was the very thing that happened. I killed off our friendship before it even got started. That day I knew I sounded like a bungling blithering idiot. I also know I didn't understand how to make a nice normal conversation after I had a few drinks. Oh the pain, the agony.

I started going to her school where they made the movie *Fame* from. It was called The School of Performing Arts. I kept going by there to see if I could make amends and be forgiven for the things I said. I remember her asking me if I wanted another chance; being the stupid dote that I was, I told her no. I did though, I wanted nothing more in this whole wide world than to be with her. I wished that we had been a couple. It could have been so great.

After a few months hanging around there, I found out she was going to have her prom. I had bought some nice clothes and decided to stop by on that wonderful night. I had my hair cut very short and laid back, smelling of this new popular cologne called Aramis, it seemed that a lot of gay guys wore this cologne, but as for me I was anything except that. The dance started about 6:00 P.M. that evening and I was in the crowd coming through the door. I looked around, and when I spotted her, I took my opportunity to try and talk to her and get a word in edgewise. The other students were all abuzz getting their frenzy on as the crowd danced up a storm. I asked Debbie if she wanted to dance with me and immediately was swarmed with her close confidants. They basically surrounded her preventing me from talking to her. When she said "No," she didn't want to dance, I looked over my shoulder to what I thought was a girl and asked her to dance; when she turned around, I realized it was a dude, my jaw dropped, and I gave up all hope. I left the dance embarrassed and full of despair.

The next few weeks seemed like a blur to me. My mother received notice that she won her Social Security claim and she decided to move out to New Jersey by my eldest brother. I still worked on the job, but things were not the same anymore. When I flew to D.C. on trips, I would come home late at night and sometimes go to work very early. I found a way to take the Amtrak train to Philadelphia and ride the subway system they had out there to a station close to my mom. So, every now and then I would go to D.C. and visit with my mother for a few hours, then head back to the city. She was happy to see me as I was to see her. When riding the train on my way back home I might pick up a pint of rum and have a drink on the train. The nights were quiet at Penn Station; most of the rush hour people were home in bed by the time I arrived. The people changed through the years, so far as the homeless and street people who were usually out there regardless of circumstances. They used to be more passive way back then, but now they seem to be so much more aggressive when trying to mingle. Who knows what has happened to society to turn out so many lost and forgotten souls, who have neither a pot to piss in, nor a window to throw it out?

I was living with my dad when my mom left New York. I stayed with him for a while until I got sick and developed pulmonary tuberculosis and became disabled for a while. I had been coughing more than usual, and I would also sweat heavily at nights; also, I started coughing up blood in my sputum. I went to the JFK hospital in Lindenwold, South Jersey and got checked out. They took a lot of tests and diagnosed me with pulmonary tuberculosis. I was shocked at first, looking to the doctors for answers, then I felt okay with it. I stayed in the hospital for a couple of weeks. I could get away from New York City and live with my mother down in South Jersey. I told my job that I was going to relocate, one reason was because I had gotten fed up with them. They promoted two other guys over me, and they expected me to be happy? I wasn't at all happy that my coworkers were promoted, and I wasn't. I think it was because they were having sex with the ladies in the firm, and I wasn't. I wanted to, but I was selective with who I had sex with. I was also too naïve and innocent. I really didn't know how to operate in a corporate setting, I had a whole lot to learn.

The hospital was nice for a while, being in isolation watching TV all day gave me some time to think about my plight. Everyday my mother would come and bring me a Philly cheesesteak hoagie with hot peppers, a bag of kettle chips, and the works. I stayed there for a couple of days and then I got discharged to my mother's place. The severity of the disease was uncommon, yet I took it in stride. Here it was me galivanting all about the country delivering packages, catching a deadly disease, and not even knowing that I was infected. Of course, I was dedicated to the job, but I hated to think I was of no value for all that I tried to do. I went to my mother's apartment thinking I would get a job and relocate to Stratford NJ. The air was fresh with plenty of bugs that saturated the environment. I was about eighteen then, having gone through such a traumatic experience that plagued my mind daily. Drinking alcohol was an easy escape route that led to more and more complications in my life. I would usually wake up in the mornings after a night of gut busting, beer slugging, glad to make it to the vomit station, the toilet. My mother rarely spoke to me about my bad behavior; she would just give me a special look to let me know she was unsatisfied with me. Whenever I read the look she gave, I would do my best to straighten up and fly right. Plenty of my days I spent with my cousin Joseph who I had grown up with. His house was in Lawnside, New Jersey; not too far from where I was staying with my mother. We would drink and get twisted in his room listening to music and trying to line up some honeys.

On a nice summer's day, he offered me an upper (Christmas Tree). I took it then I told him I couldn't feel it. Then I asked him for a few more, maybe five or so and I took them too. We went out to a party for a while, then the uppers started to kick in. My stomach felt like a motor was running fast, so I asked him to take me home. He agreed; while on the way we stopped at a convenience store and picked up a gallon of milk. I don't know how I thought of that, but it worked. I was not only a teenage alcoholic, but also a pill popper, at least for that time I was. I woke up later that day after throwing up all the pills I ingested with the alcohol, and I felt like shit. I swore if I got through it this time I would never drink again.

I stayed clean for about thirty days then something annoyed me, and I used it as an excuse to start back drinking. One of the reasons that I drank so much was because of the people I hung around; seemed like everybody around me drank or smoked weed. It could have been okay on a different basis, but I became more involved than I should have. When I realized what I was doing I didn't know how to stop, or which way to go from there. I fell into a rut of drinking and hanging with people who weren't about anything. I stayed there for almost two years until my older brother that lived in New York asked me to come back and help him out. I didn't want to leave but I had become a burden on my mother, and I couldn't find a job. For many months I walked up and down the roadways searching for one, however, I did luck up at a McDonalds flipping burgers for a month or two, but I soon lost that job. Also, my so-called friend helped me get another one at a gas station, which was fine until he sabotaged the business saying my books were off. He was probably in hock to somebody else and was desperate for cash. When the boss came in and saw the figures, he fired me. This was a real pisser; I couldn't win for losing; seems like everything I touched turned to shit with no one to give me good counsel.

I made it back to Brooklyn to a place my brother gave me in his house on Green Ave. I was staying in the attic; it was nice and cozy by myself, I had to go to the next lower floor to cook and use the bathroom. Me and my brother would go out at night to find things to sell to the secondhand store. They would give us a few dollars for the things we found. The prices fluctuated but not by much. My brother and I drank beers and snorted cocaine on our downtime. The work wasn't too hard, it's just that it didn't lead to anything promising. The attic was filled with nude pics plastered on the walls and ceiling. This was no way to try and relax after working, those pretty figures always left me wondering if there were any real women in my life that looked as good. Hell, any girl looked good after a few beers and a snort.

Our days usually started about 3:00 or 4:00 A.M. in the morning, going in the streets to find things others had no longer any use for. It never really hit me as something beneath me for a line of work, I just didn't pay it any mind. After we finished, we would take the stuff to the secondhand store and barter for the best prices. My brother was fair though, he gave me a portion of the values. His wife also made good food who happened to be Korean. I really cared for her throughout the years; she stuck with my brother, and they raised a lovely family. From there I started helping the secondhand store owner during the days and at night I chilled out at the house. My brother had a talk with the owner who ran the nightclub on Broadway who gave me a job there as a DJ. His name was Jocko, and he was well known in the city. He sold coke on the side and offered exotic dancers for entertainment in the club. Most of the time I was having fun, running up a tab and enjoying the people. I stayed there for a while under the same routine until this one evening when this dancer named Gina was on stage; she was popping that pussy just right, enough to throw me off kilter. Her body was calling me right into the back room where the dancers congregated. I went back behind the partition and the dancers were freebasing. They asked me if I wanted to try it, so I said "Okay," not knowing what this was going to lead to. They took some cocaine, baking soda, mixed it with some water and cooked it. When it finished cooking the person took it and poured some cold water on it to help it solidify. They broke off a little chunk and put it in a glass pipe. After taking a drag they passed it to me and I inhaled it, then blew out the smoke. I didn't really feel anything in that moment. I went back to the stage where I was playing the music and put on some more selections. Keeping the people satisfied with the music was not that hard because I had a lot of good music to play. Even if I didn't have something, I was able to borrow music from the other DJ's stash with his permission. No matter what I did I always took care of other people's property. After a few more drinks Gina came back out and started shaking her nice little ass; watching her seemed to put me in a trance and I knew I wanted some of her stuff. I stood there on stage watching all the other dancers that performed, but to me, she was the best.

After the party ended and it was time to go, I asked Jocko for half a gram of coke to cook and try to smoke some more. He gave it to me and then I left for the streets; the sunlight awoke my senses as I moved from the dark club to the outside. I lived around the corner so I just went home to my space and asked my other brother to help me cook the coke so we could smoke. He finished and put in a nice chunk for me to try; this time it was different for me. I got dizzy to the point of almost passing out, then it sounded like bells and whistles and jet engines taking off. I bent over for a minute and slowly gathered my composure. "Wow, that shit is good," I said to myself, slightly sweating and amazed at the experience I just had. Then I took another hit and like the first one, it was almost the same. I got a surge of power pulsating through my veins. We finished off what I had, drank some more beers and I finally fell asleep. I woke up late and got ready for work; not thinking about what I had done earlier that day. My mouth was dry, and I could have used a drink. Tonight, was going to be a regular night, with no dancers which was not as much fun. Later, after playing it was time to get paid. I had used a large portion of my pay buying drinks and snorting coke, so I only had a few dollars left which I was not too happy about.

When I left, I went to a crack house on Palmetto St. to get a few jumbos, or nickels to smoke. I might have had about $50 to spend for that session as soon as I approached the street there were crackheads scattered all about the area trying to find a way to get high. They always had a story, a song, and a dance for why you should help them. I rarely thought about what they were saying, I just wanted to get my stuff and enjoy the high, which didn't happen often. That's the reason I stayed to myself most of the time; those crackheads always fucked my head up with their simple-minded shit. Crack can make a person do the most outrageous things you can think of. One of the things I resent so much is believing in one of them in any circumstances; in other words, falling far their bullshit. One of the lookouts might tell me to give them something until they got paid later when the boss comes and pays them. I might get on the block about 12:00 noon and be waiting for them to return the favor at 10:00 P.M. that night. When and if they get paid, they never could find me even if I'm two feet away. It's the whole greasy nature of some people that made getting high such a drag. There would be so many negative scenarios a person can experience; overall it makes the high so not worth it. Especially the damage it does to families and their loved ones.

So, I was at the crack house dressed in my blue wool pinstriped suit, smoking lovely all day until towards the night there's a loud knock on the door; it's Five 'O, the cops. Everybody starts running for an escape, and I run to the top floor. I say to myself that I'm not going to jail, and I must find a way out. I looked at the distance from the building we were in and the one next door; it wasn't too far so I got it in my head that I can jump over to the other side. I reached out my hands and grasped onto the ledge. I grabbed the other building, but now I was dangling from the roof top four stories up from the ground. I managed to pull myself over the ledge and I kneeled looking over the edge surreptitiously. There was still a commotion down on the street and in the building, I climbed over from. I stood there wondering how in the hell I got myself into that position. Almost thirty minutes later I heard the cops leaving and I didn't know who or what was happening inside the crack house. I think I still had a few dollars left and I bought a few more hits and finally, I went out on the streets.

I was broke now and I still wanted to get high; I looked at some cans in the street which were worth a few pennies. I didn't think of how many I needed to get something, so I just started to pick them up. In a little time, my hands had become dirty and greasy; this was truly not going to work, and I had to find a better way to achieve my objective. I started asking people for some help with change if they could spare it. This was much quicker and cleaner, after all, I hated getting my hands filthy so collecting bottles and cans was totally out of the question for me. I always had to stay clean when I was getting high it was a habit; didn't like people looking at me funny, especially if they knew me. I stayed dipping and dabbling with drugs and alcohol; one to lift me up, and the other to bring me down.

As I was walking from the crack house up Broadway on a cool dark evening, I noticed some guys walking down the street with some stuff in their hands. They had just broken into a record store coming out with things and it was still open. I didn't think twice about going in as I was totally broke. I had never done anything like this before and didn't know what to expect. I climbed up the store fence outside the store and pulled myself through the air conditioner's space that was removed. It was dark inside, and I was fumbling around a little, then I used my lighter to see what was inside. Almost two minutes inside another guy climbed through the hole, I thought to myself, we might be able to work together and come off. Well five minutes later in there I was ready to leave, and I told the guy to let us get whatever we had and go. He looked at me and just kept on looking for stuff; he said he wanted to gather a complete sound system, and that's when I immediately said to myself, "This dumb bastard done lost his mind, I'm outer here."

I started throwing stuff out the window to gather when I hit the ground when I climbed back out, and then I looked down, and some of the stuff I was throwing hit a police car parked underneath the hole. I told the guy that they were outside, and we had to find a way out. He looked at me dumbfounded and started to look for an exit. We both realized that there was only one way in and one way out. As we went towards the back of the store there was a hidden room which we found by pushing a door-like structure. We both went in and tried to be extra quiet.

The SWAT team cut through the steel fence and was inside with some dogs. They yelled, "You better come out now or we are going to start shooting through the wall," and we also heard the sniffer dogs waiting to get in and find us hiding.

I told them, "Hold up, I'm coming out."

I slowly opened the partition and came out of the hidden secret room. One of the SWAT team came forth and poked me in the belly with an assault rifle while my hands were up in the air. He said," You better tell me the truth, is anybody else in there?"

I told him "Yeah, there's one more guy in there." This dumb motherfucker was trying to hide under a pile of newspapers he had pulled on top of himself, then they let the dog loose and told him to get him. A few seconds later the guy started yelling and hollering, "Okay, I'm coming out now, get your dog, Ooh, Ooh, Oou, Oou, stop." When he came through the door they smacked the shit out of him and then hit him with a barrage of punches and maybe a few kicks. Then they took us both through the store door which was now open and pushed us into the squad car. My head was spinning, and I wished I had not been caught in this situation. Some of the people from the crack house saw us being placed in custody and they shook their heads.

The precinct was only three blocks away, so this was an easy collar for them. The arresting officers were reluctant to touch us and kept their distance. When we reached inside, the precinct we were told to remove our shoelaces and belts for security reasons. They had arrested two other guys that were outside I didn't know about, who might have been associated with the other defendant. They started showing they knew each other and kept trying to tell me not to snitch. I said to myself, "What the fuck are they saying?" I don't know you and I did what I did on my own, so don't try and tell me anything, just leave me out of your bullshit. We stayed there for almost thirty hours until Central Bookings was ready to receive us. In the meantime, I was so hungry, then they fed us an egg sandwich which I was so happy to get. For the guys that had money on them, they could ask the officers to get them snacks from the vending machines by their front desk. Sitting on the concrete floor thinking about all the trouble I was in made it hard for me to sleep. Somehow after laying there, going over it, over and over in my head I finally allowed myself to get some rest. One shift came in to replace the other and we were all still waiting to go to the next steps in the process.

It must have been about 7:00 P.M. when they finally called me and my co-defendants to get chained up for the ride Downtown Brooklyn, where Central Bookings was located. The van was packed with people standing, and some sitting. Wherever you were in the truck you had to stay there until you got to the destination. I and the detainees formed a line to exit the bus and stood in place as was instructed by the accompanying officers. The police department had an extensive system of protocol for dealing with detainees. Everything had a purpose and a reason and was therefore always under intense scrutiny. As we disembarked the vehicle we were ushered to an entrance where the officers had to relinquish their weapons. Then the door buzzed, and we were allowed to enter the holding pen areas. In each section or area different things went on; the first being pedigreed, which is making sure that each person is matched to their paperwork or file. Then came the strip search; taking off all your clothes and showing the officers your private parts to make sure you were not in possession of contraband. Sometimes prisoners had drugs, crack pipes, weapons, cigarettes, or even cash that was not taken at the initial arrest precinct. If they found it at the Bookings, they might give you another charge for having it. In the 1980s, freebasing and crack-using reached epidemic proportions. This led to the jails being filled with all kinds of cases stemming from drug usage. So, when you got to a bullpen at first there might be a seat for you on a bench, then that may have gotten too crowded, or your butt was so sore from sitting that you tried and find some space on the floor to sit. Then that space became so filled that you had to stand in one spot until you found an area to lay your head. You could get sleep until you are awakened by a fight between somebody who wanted to try another person, or the space is so limited that somebody cracks under the pressure. The jails were filled with mostly African Americans and Puerto Ricans then other nationalities.

So, after waiting four or five days I got to see the court worker who gathered my personal information that was to go before the judge, enlightening them of the person I am, who was to stand before the court to be prosecuted. Thinking to myself that it was my first offense so I should be able to go free, but then many career criminals offer their advice; (jail-house lawyers). Sometimes they can help with certain information, but it is never anything written in stone. At times what they say is applicable, while at other times their info is useless. That is one reason lawyers may get paid so much, they must know as many angles of the law as possible. You would think when a person must utilize their service you would get the best they have to offer; not always true.

As I entered the bullpen, which was usually filled to the brim, I noticed the framework of the construction in each place I had the opportunity to scrutinize. Every nut, bolt, plate of steel, wire, light, door, or window was designed and reinforced to keep us from escaping. The impact of where you are begins to seep in painting a picture of gloom and despair; heaven forbid if you are claustrophobic or suffer from any other psychological disorder. After sitting in limbo for a few hours, it is possible to imbed every inch of a cell into the memory. Just sitting and waiting for the opportunity to see the Judge is what most every thought is concentrated on; some handling it better than others. The sounds of the gates opening in the next cell catch my attention; slowly making their way over to us is the feed-up crew. The main staple is bologna and cheese sandwiches, then if they gave me some Kool-Aid or milk to go with it, I was okay. Some of the guys would not even look at those sandwiches, let alone eat one. As hungry as I was, I asked them for theirs if they didn't want to eat it or ask the COs for another if they can spare it. Most of the time they didn't mine giving out extras just if everyone ate first. After eating and my belly full, now I could rest better, then I would somehow manage to fall asleep. A little later the guard comes in and moves me to another cell, this one right next to the courtroom. You could hear the court in session; the bailiff calling the dockets and the Prosecutor droning on about how the criminal is a threat to society.

"Mr. Rabinowitz, Mr. Rabinowitz, where are you?" The courtroom officer started searching for one of the detainees, looking around the bull pen with a picture and file in hand, gazing over the sea of faces. Not being able to distinguish those on the floor and benches he again called out,

"Mr. Rabinowitz, Heimlich Rabinowitz, where are youuuu?" From under a bench with old newspapers pulled on top of himself, he came from his spot and answered the call,

"I'm over here-yaa." A small figure of a man dusty with his hair disheveled wearing a black wool jacket, he navigated over the bodies shewn about the floor. He went into the booth with his lawyer, and they discussed his case. He then came out and waited for them to call his name in the courtroom. A few minutes later they came in and called my name, I then went through the same process. They called me to the courtroom, and I stood before the judge.

"Mr. Davis, you were caught in the act of committing a burglary in the Third Degree, in violation of such and such of the Penal Code, how do you plead?"

"I plead guilty your honor."

"Well, Mr. Davis, we want you to implicate your codefendants." Then my lawyer leaned over to me and said, "The judge wants you to say that you were acting in concert with your codefendants to commit this crime."

"We were not acting together. I only met that guy after I had already went in the record store, then we were supposed to be working together, but when I saw that the dude lost his mind and bugged out, I started to leave that's when I through the stuff on the street, and was going to escape, but got caught."

"Your honor, he doesn't want to do it." She was a nasty short Jewish bitch, ready to hark spit across the room into my face; she said, "All right then, come back to court in two months, you are released on your own recognizance." Then my court-appointed lawyer told me to go and stay out of trouble, but to make sure I come back to court on the date issued. When I heard that it was the best news which made my day, I left the courthouse feeling like a million; even though I didn't even have the carfare to get home. I left 120 Schermerhorn Street and headed for the subway, they gave me a token to get on the train, I made it back home and took a good look at where my life had come to. Of course, I could say I was embarrassed and knew this wasn't where I wanted to be, but I had a long, long journey to be completed before I would start to change.

My brother was buying the house on Greene Ave from my father; he had gone into the service and was able to get a loan from the Veterans Administration. I don't know if that was how he was going to pay for it, but they had their differences. They didn't agree completely on a few things, there was bad blood between them. Eventually my brother moved out of the house far away to another state. By this time, my mother moved back to New York also; she was staying with my younger sister. I had been out of work from the law firm for a while and I wanted to work and do better, so I got a job with Trans America on Madison Ave as a messenger.

I worked there for about six months, and my father started to nag me when I was at home. "Johnnie, you better get your ass up and go to work. I'll be damned if I'm going to take care of you." I might be hung over from the night before, but I never neglected to go to work. I would be so tired that I would barely stay awake. I would sometimes buy some coke and sniff it while I was working. There was a door attendant, porter who might take a toot with me. I also drank quite a bit of Asti Spumante wine, or beer to take off the edge. I was holding on narrowly, then my younger sister told me I could come and live with her and my mother. This was cool for me, so I stayed with them for about a year. There was a young lady downstairs that always seemed to come and give me a genuinely nice greeting, "Heyyy Johnnie."

"Hi Vye, what's going on?" I didn't notice that she was sweet on me at first, then I started to notice her more, then one night it happened. We had a long talk, she told me her baby's daddy had gotten himself killed and she was raising her daughter by herself. Vye was short for Vyanne Schofield; she was a cute, me-dium-sized, brown-skinned beauty with a nice round fat ass that had more bounce to the ounce. While I didn't immediately try to hit on her, I noticed her more as time went on while I stayed in their house. She was the landlord's daughter, who worked for the post office for plenty of years. The house was a brownstone right in the center of Bedford Stuyvesant on Handcock Street and Lewis Ave. She had two younger brothers that stayed there also on the lower floors. They kept a nice clean house and stayed mostly to themselves. I seemed to be the only one that broached their circle of friends or associates.

On a regular day I would get up and walk to the train Station on Fulton Street and Utica Ave, it stayed busy all the time. Then I would take the train to Trans America to walk the streets of the city. Sometimes I had to argue to get the tokens for the trips with the supervisor; he was a younger white guy that impressed me with his ability to manage the business for his people. He was usually there in the morning before I came in and had most of the stops laid out for me to take when I arrived. Sometimes I had to deliver letters or packages by the Red-Light District on 42nd Street and 8th Ave. On an average day, guys selling crack would be in the area trying to hustle; this became an opportunity for me to get high while I was around. I might take a hit and regret it after I did, knowing I still had to finish working and I would be torn between the work and the urge to get high. I just did it occasionally when I first started out, then slowly it progressed over time. I would work all week, then I was supposed to receive my pay it was too small, constantly. I was bitter working all the time needing to make more money than I was getting. After passing a Popeyes Fast Food on Seventh Ave in Mid-Town, I saw some good looking high yellow girls working a counter and decided to try and get a job working there, as a second job. I went in and spoke to one of the managers who told me to come back on another day when the big boss was there. I did and he hired me for the late shift. I would work from 9 A.M. to 5 P.M. on one job, then work from 6 P.M. till 2 A.M. on the other. I would be so tired when I got off at night that I could barely make it home. The trains ran once every hour, and if I missed it, I had to wait for the next train to come on the schedule. So, for the next few weeks I became acclimated to the process of making that good Louisiana Cajun Chicken. A little Indian guy with an accent spoke to me occasionally, but there was a language barrier. He wanted to properly school me on the technique of how to prepare the best fried chicken.

From the start the chicken used was superior to the ones bought at a regular grocery store or supermarket. Cases of Kosher Empire chicken, nice-looking, clean, packed with ice and fresh to the smell. I had to take the chicken out of the bags which had the pieces from four chickens each, the legs, thighs, wings, and breast no necks and gizzards were included. Then they were rinsed and placed in buckets with mild or spicy seasoning, marinated and put in the refrigerators for 24 hours. Then it was ready to cook, in a special grease that had to be cleaned frequently. There were distinct agents added to the grease to make it stable longer also cleaner too. Sometimes the workers would sneak and eat a piece here and there, but as for me I only came to work. At the end of the night, we had to clean all the equipment, the floors, and the lobby. When we finished if there was any food left over, they would give it to us to take home. I used to take it for my mother, sister, and my niece. We all loved it because the food was great, especially the Cajun style red beans and rice.

When I got off on those late nights, I would stop by Vyanne's house and knock on her door; she would let me in and give me some of her good, good pussy. It's like she had my dick trained for more and more, no matter how tired I was, it was never an issue once I arrived in her arms. She meant something to me for a while, but just like all things, nothing lasts forever. Her fat juicy pussy would pucker up like a blooming flower, and I beat it down like a jackhammer. I loved to hear her moan, "Ohh Johnnie," she called out while her eyes rolled in the back of her head. "Yeah Baby, you good pussy motherfucker." This went on for a few months until she started going awry. My sister's boyfriend started hitting it behind my back, she had some other guys she snuck around with also. I didn't know anything for sure, but I followed the signs; I saw where her personality changed and, in my mind, and heart, I knew she was cheating. I didn't know how to manage it at first, so I just acted like everything was all right, eventually withdrawing slowly from her intimacy. I stopped having sex with her and then showing no interest in being with her. Before I sealed the deal quitting her altogether, I took her to see a George Benson, Roberta Flack concert. When we got there, we sat down and I noticed her trying to get her hoe on, so I left my seat. Before I did, I gave her a pen so she could get the guy's number if she wanted to. I felt so miserable when I left there that I couldn't wait to get back home. Things were never the same, but I didn't care anymore. To me she was trash, just like the other women in my life who never reciprocated half the love and concern I showed for them. That's just the way the cookie crumbles.

As time went on, I stayed out increasingly into the wee hours of the morning.

I remember losing objects, looking in the gutters for the belongings I lost, mostly because I was in such a hurry or because so many things plague my mind. I didn't deserve this, but what could I do. My mother began to stay up at night waiting for me to come home. She couldn't sleep knowing I was out there in the streets, and anything could have happened to me. Many times, when I reached home, I could see where she had been crying her precious eyes out, they were bloodshot-red I knew she wanted me to see this, but I didn't respond correctly to her feelings, to her needs. It was as though I didn't care, I was supposed to stop getting high, hanging out in the streets, and come home to get some rest. I felt like shit when this happened over and over. I should have just sought help or tried to change but I didn't until it was too late.

My behavior changed overnight; I stopped working regularly and when I got paid, I didn't give my sister her fair share of the rent. I always had excuses until she got fed up and we had a falling-out. Eventually I started staying in the streets longer than I was at home till I finally gave up, and this wreaked havoc on my family life.

I didn't make a lot of money, but I didn't spend time together with Vye or see other women on the side at first when I thought everything was fine, and to my dismay, she started having sex with everybody in my circle besides me. I thought she was trifling, that's all. She wasn't the first and neither was she the last. Most of my life I tried to be the best guy I could be when it came to relationships; it just wasn't in the cards for me to be the good guy, so later for all that good guy crap. Sometimes I asked myself what I was doing wrong to make women turn on me? Then I stopped caring to know because it no longer mattered.

Eventually my sister left from there and my mom moved in with my other sister up on Hancock Street and Nostrand Ave. My memory serves me vaguely; can't remember all the times and places it's my mind being selective on what it wants to reveal, however the culmination of my life span was a wasteful flop without any concrete meaning.

I had been going back and forth to court for 11 months on that burglary charge when the warrant squad picked me up. The judge had given me five years' probation and she claimed she told me if she saw me in front of her again, she would sentence me to one to three years in a state prison. I had to report to the probation office for the initial visit. I asked the people there in that office when I was supposed to come back for my scheduled meetings. I was told they would let me know; that was the last time I saw or heard from them. So, I went in front of the judge, and she is bent all out of shape for seeing me, then my lawyer just turned his head, stepped aside and abandoned me. I explained to him that I was waiting for the probation department to contact me when I was picked up. No matter what was said, it was to no avail, the only thing they were concerned with was filling another state prison bed. Its ashamed that the law proceeds that way against mostly black people and the prison system is predicated on filling prisons with people not necessarily involved in the actual crime.

"Mister Davis, didn't I tell you that the next time I saw your face in this courtroom I would sentence you to a one-to-three-year term?"

"Your honor, I went to the probation department like you told me, and they said they were going to contact me when to come in. They never did and I was waiting for them to do that, it just never happened."

"Take the defendant into custody, you are hereby sentenced to the term of one to three years in a state prison determined by the Department of Corrections."

"What, your honor. Your honor, I was never contacted." As I stood there trying to explain my circumstances the bailiff took me into custody and my lawyer, walked the other way as if he never even met me a day in my life. Maybe later that night when he was eating dinner or having some drinks with friends; he could say to his conscious that he helped the system put away another nigger. The communities up-state New York must've given them a kick back for the number of prisoners they sent to their prisons. Not one bit of sleep did they lose over placing me in prison and ruining my life. So, for the next years I had to find a way to reduce the effects of acquiring a prison record. There were so many detainees on Rikers Island that we had to wait to be shipped up-state, there were no beds for the system to handle us all.

On Rikers Island my first time in jail was an eye-opening experience. The worst part from the beginning was being in the bullpens again; dirty, stinking, smelly, prisoners strewn about the floors, laying in filth, just coming off the streets. We stayed in them for a couple of days moving from cell to cell, until we were finally housed. When we did get to a house the other prisoners let you know right away you had to jump in the showers, they didn't allow people in their housing areas off the streets stinking and smelly. This raised red flags immediately if you ever heard stories about the jailhouse. The showers are where guys got fucked in the ass if they were not strong enough to fight off an attacker. I heard stories about it, but I didn't experience it, at least for my prison bids. When they approached me with the deal, I was happy to get in the shower because it had been a long while since I had taken a bath. So, as I got in and proceeded to wash when this gay guy spoke like he wanted to do something. I took up a fighting stance ready to attack, he then backed off, after he threatened to hit me with a mop ringer, but it never came to that. I finished and went to my bed area. Later, I fell asleep and didn't wake up till an early morning hour when a bell rang. It was the bell letting us know to get ready for breakfast (Chow). It was about 5:30 A.M.; this was the time we had to get up in the morning if you wanted to eat. For me I didn't have much of a choice because I stayed hungry most of the time I spent locked up, and I always had a good appetite. I didn't gain much weight when I first started going to prison, but I did when I started working out up-state.

The first time on Rikers Island back in 1987, I started out going to the mess hall early in the morning volunteering to help in the dining area. I figured I might get a job eventually to help me by some commissary, that's what most of the other guys did so I followed suit. The first position they gave me was called tabletops. This is wiping down the tables after the detainees had eaten, sweeping up, mopping the floors when the feeding was finished. The officers allowed us to bring back certain foods when we were going back to the cells or dormitories. The work was therapeutic taking your mind off things. Being around the kitchen gave me a sense of fulfilment, like I was doing something of value. As time moved forward, I began to spend more time in the kitchens until they gave me a job working for them. At my overnight job when I started work at 11:00 P.M. and stayed till the feeding was over in the morning; when the time finished I began staying longer, and longer. When I would go back to the housing area there were a couple of guys that I would work out with. We would do push-ups and dips till we burned out. This became a daily routine for a while until some of them went away because their time was up, and other times they went up-state to continue their bids.

One morning the captain of the officer's mess hall asked me if I would like to work for the KK. This was the place where the staff ate; I said "sure," and I was in like Flint. From the time I started working in the kitchens, I learned things and changed physically and mentally. I became a more rounded, or seasoned individual. It had been almost 11months when I got a notice I was going to leave on the next bus upstate. I thought about all the friends I made and not knowing what to expect for the next leg of my journey, it felt good to have such a sense of accomplishment. When night fell, I was a bit nervous when the morning came, I had to go to the mess hall again for the last time. All the servers behind the line were saddened to see me leaving and they tried to give me anything they could food wise to show their respect. I too felt a sense of loss but knew it was only the beginning of a new story.

We all stood around waiting for the transport team to call our names. When they finally got to me, I was glad to get linked up and go. They used handcuffs and long chains that went all the way to my ankle; the chain ran around my back and chest, pulling it close to the wrists. It was so uncomfortable that when I finally arrived at Downstate Correctional Facility I was greatly relieved, "Thank God." The cuffs came off, then it was smooth processing us into the facility. The C.O. began the spiel about the dos and don'ts of being there, almost yelling so there was no question whether you heard them or not. Just as soon as he finished one of the guys thought he was still on Rikers Island and began to act out. In two seconds about four big hillbilly gruff C.O.s pounced on him; when they were finished, he was out cold lying on the floor. They used that moment to make an example of the poor guy, guess he thought he was tough. Most of the other inmates fell in line not wanting to cause any problems. One of the first things they did was take our body measurements and then sent us to take a cool shower; they also gave us a special shampoo to wash with to kill lice and bugs we might have. There was no taking chances with the new admissions, they could have any number of stowaways hiding on their skin. So, when we finished, got dressed and proceeded to the next station.

The processing took a couple of days to complete so the next thing we did was go to our assigned housing unit. When we arrived, we were told to lock our cells. The cells were small rooms with a bed and toilet and four walls to stare at. As I looked on the walls there was writing scribbled all around the cell from guys who had been there throughout the years. Their names, graffiti tags or the year they were there plastered the scenery. When one had more experience, they left a drawing which could have been quite seasoned. So many brothers came through those doors being at odds with society, some for other reasons which may or may not have been justified. The night fell slowly as I peered out the small-sized window offering a stingy view; the sounds of the other inmates lightly coated the drab occasion. During the night, the pangs of hunger groped my belly as I wished for another piece of the bread and butter from dinner to satisfy it. The minutes turned into hours while my mind refused to rest or let my body take sleep. Eventually I fell asleep, just in time to wake up for breakfast, just in time to take another step further in a phase of rehabilitation. The first sounds you would hear in the morning were the officers coming in for the change of shift. The night officers informed the day shift of any significant changes and gave them the count. The officer will then proceed to count the prisoners and make sure they are still there and alive. To my surprise some guys just refuse to accept being locked up and move to hang themselves. For myself this wasn't an option, I've always found it hard to do something against me, even though when I was doing drugs and alcohol, I was doing the exact same thing. The officer finishes the count and informs us to be ready for chow at a specified time.

As we sat patiently for the signal, the mess hall contacted the block to send us down to eat. We line up as if we were in the military, ramrod straight looking ahead in a silent mode. At Downstate you could hear a pin drop as we walked through the winding tunnels, which they and the whole complex was made of concrete and reinforced steel. It looked like a scene out of a movie, not sure which one but one that was famous. After entering the cafeteria, I start looking around for any familiar faces. Every now and then I might spot someone I knew from the city but that was a rare occasion. Most of the guys that were there didn't have anyone to fraternize with, they had to make new associates or in some cases friends. The food was a life saver though; it was important to have enough to eat, it usually took away some of the misery. The meals were consistent: six slices of bread in the mornings with jelly, milk, coffee, juice, and the cereals were different every day. Other times pancakes or French toast might be served with sausages and eggs. They didn't play around with the food after the Attica riots. The entire system changed because of them; they helped prisoners get their human rights that was being denied across the state. The prison conditions were deplorable up until then. In the modern prison life, things seemed to be much more livable.

After eating breakfast, we would return to our cells and wait to be further processed. There was a series of intake steps that were necessary before going to the next facility. There were many classifications different for everyone based on certain criteria. For instance, hard core criminals that were prone to act up were placed in facilities with the same kind of inmates; however, the general population housed a variety of inmates from both ends of the spectrum, from hard to soft. So, on a regular day we were group assessed to see what level of education we were on and to see how much help it will take to have us rehabilitated. The main thing that could have helped to save our lives would have been to give us a job, self-worth, and a means to fulfil our destiny, the one we chose, not the one thrust upon us. As I readied myself, in front of the state monitor I noticed it was for math tests. I knew a small amount to get me through the basic questions, but I hadn't excelled that subject in school. I sat down and went through the exercises briefly, when I finished testing the monitor screwed up my paper and I got the wrong score. Then we went back to the unit and got ready for lunch. This went on for about two weeks, also after the first week we were able to lock out at night and watch the television. The C.O. controlled the remote, so we had to agree on something first and then he would put it on; unlike back on Rikers Island. Back there, guys with too many issues always screwed things up when they tried to dominate either the TV or the telephones. They acted like they brought them with them from their houses. I never gravitated towards jailhouse politics, I either sat down and watched the program on the TV or found something else to do. The first time I went to Downstate Correctional Facility, it took a month to get classified and shipped out to the next place, then in the later times it was a much shorter process.

The first facility I transferred to was at Watertown, New York, close to Canada. The place had the right name too; it seemed to snow or rain most of the seasons I stayed there. The ride was hell on my butt, and very uncomfortable with the handcuffs and shackles. We stopped at a few other facilities before we arrived at Watertown, given lunch and made the best of the ride. When I finally arrived, there were other inmates sprawled about the compound, they looked at the bus load of new inmates like we were fresh meat. Watertown was a medium level correctional facility, which afforded us a bit more freedom than a Max Prison. The beds were placed in barrack-like structures classed as dormitories.

The insides looked exceptionally clean in comparison to the jails from the city. Every inmate had a cubical of their own, which might have a double bunk (two beds). Each block usually had one or two COs on duty who were the big chief of that unit at that time. The sergeants passed and inspected the units regularly for compliance. There were many things an inmate could do to pass the time, such as reading, playing cards, exercising, cooking, watching TV or just taking a walk in the yard. It wasn't fun all the time; at inopportune moments fights broke out or somebody got stabbed, this rarely happened in most places when it did, they locked down the whole prison.

After I settled in for the first few days, I went to the program committee; they asked me what job I wanted to do, I told them I wanted to go in the welding program. The committee rep looked at my test scores from Downstate and told me my score wasn't high enough, I disputed with him to no avail, they gave me horticulture and small engine repair. That's the way it was throughout most of my life, I wanted to do something, and some jackass wouldn't let me because they had they final say. So, during the weekdays I went to those classes, and the weekends I had to myself. There were times I sat on the porch outside my unit, where big flies buzzed along the perimeter. One day one of them flew right in my mouth. I was so surprised that they could be so bold and aggressive. A few months went by, then I enrolled in the handicrafts course; we made many different things. Then afterwards I began to engage in weightlifting and exercising. Most of the guys who had been down for a while developed a routine; for the cal-isthenics we did push-ups, pull-ups, and dips. After a few months of working out, a guy could start to look buff, for me it was just an okay physique, nothing spectacular. Some of the other inmates lived for their workouts. They wanted to attract and seduce women when they were released. For me it was just something to do before I got back in society at home. While I was there I received visits from my mother and father. The prisons had a program where the families of inmates were able to visit on certain days by riding their designated buses.

After spending nine months in this facility, I was granted the Work Release Program. Earlier the previous month I received a letter stating that I made the list, and then that day came when they packed me up to go. They sent me to Queensboro Correctional Facility by the Queensboro Bridge in New York City. The area was commercial having little to no private houses for a long distance. I never ventured into the neighborhoods, staying to the path that led to and from the facility. It took a few weeks before I was able to go out on furlough, that's when you can spend time with your family. Most of the guys had girlfriends or wives that they would go home to. The next step in the process was to get a job, then after that all the doors started opening. They gave us time to go out and look for a job, but it had to be legit though, it couldn't be that you could go and hang out with your homeboy all day hustling on the side and catch an added charge. They were aware of the pathetic pitfalls and took every precautionary measure to prevent it.

In the day I spent most of my time by the kitchen helping the cooks again, they also appreciated me because I made their job easier. When the feeding was done, they allowed me to take some food back; I would make sandwiches and sell them for 2 or 3 dollars each. This was nice at first, but I wanted more, I did this for a while and then things changed.

I was granted a 12-hour pass to look for a job, so that day I went to 34th Street in Manhattan, by 7th Ave and passed by a McDonalds. I filled out the application then walked down the street to a Wendy's. I spoke to the manager and asked him for a job, he looked at me and gave me his approval. He told me to come back on a Thursday for orientation so that's what I did. I was so happy to have landed one so quickly, thinking myself lucky because most of the guys back at the facility found it extremely hard to get a job. I went back to the facility and placed a request to see my parole officer. He had to approve the job before I could get an ongoing pass to go daily. He spoke with me, and I filled out some paperwork giving him more details of the prospective job. Everything was fine now; I was on my way back to normalcy. That night I called my people and told them the good news; they were delighted.

That Thursday came quickly as I took the E train to the 34th Street stop, people were moving in a rush mostly to their respective destinations. Others took their time taking in the sites, enjoying the scenery, spending cash, and talking in foreign languages. Tourist saturated the region surrounding Madison Square Garden and were well received by the hospitality community. I sat in the dining room at Wendy's for a few minutes before the hiring manager came and started calling people to interview them. When he came to me, he asked me about my availability and my past experiences. I told him of the time I spent at

Popeyes and Rikers Island. He seemed impressed and told me when to start.

That Monday when I arrived someone explained to me that I was going to be working on the outside cleaning the tables and dumping the garbage cans, this was fine I thought. Another thing I should mention is the pay was above minimum wage, $4.15 an hour. This made me feel even better. After two weeks they called me to work behind the line; the place was extraordinary. A whole lot of yelling and dropping fries, flipping burgers, making shakes, and feeding hungry people. On an average day we must have fed about three thousand people between 10:30 A.M. to 4:00 P.M. I can say that I'm exaggerating but I know we fed a lot of people, we got them in, and we got them out. When the doors closed each day, it felt like a good workout. Everyone knew they did a wonderful job. There came a time when I was making the baked potatoes and I stop waiting for the people to order, I just dropped a big load and adjusted the speed as I saw the size of the line, anticipating the demand. This made the boss happy because we were beginning to have more than enough to manage the crowd. After a few weeks I became acclimated and took a trip down the street to a Sbarro's. The place was immaculate, selling fine Italian food, or so I thought it was, also pizza. I went in and asked to fill out an application, the boss gave it to me and a week later I was working there. I told my PO, and he was amazed with my progress. He approved and I felt good that I was making a good impression on him. By this time, I was staying back at my father's house. I started working as a busser cleaning tables and washing dishes. The store was adjacent to the IRT subway system on 7th Ave. The garbage was stored downstairs in that area, so at night I had to drag the bags of garbage up the stairs and put them out. When the big boss Jerry Sbarro came through with his folk, I would show them nice hospitality. You can tell they enjoyed my servitude and respect. He was nice and clean cut, with olive colored skin with the look of a European heir.

Everyday those dishes got cleaner and cleaner, and I would spend time watching the cooks make the Italian dishes. Just like any fast-food operation they had a method; I had a passion for learning new things in the kitchen, however I couldn't learn all the cooking techniques they had to offer. I did learn to twirl some pizza though and I helped with the calzones. Later, I moved up to be the steam table operator, this was right up my ally. The cook showed me how to heat up the food and to plate it. There was an immense pleasure serving people from around the world and being a well-groomed Sbarro representative. I served the customers with a nice courteous smile with a pleasant greeting. They liked my style because they kept coming back. The regulars came at lunchtime for the pizza with the special toppings, and the tourist usually came at night with their families. No kidding the food was very tasty and elevated above regular fast food, well worth the difference in price.

I was allowed to eat spaghetti, or pizza for my lunch; I would usually put a chicken cutlet under the spaghetti topped with mozzarella and sauce. When the doors closed at night, my job was to put up the leftover foods and polish the brass railings. After an entire day of touching the railings, they became smudged down with fingerprints which clearly called for restoration to a pristine sparkle. The next on the list was the floor had to be swept and mopped. When everything was done, I grabbed some food, nothing big and a slice of blueberry cheesecake. Every now and then I would give my food to a homeless person. I didn't stick around to see them eat it, but I knew they could really enjoy it, as I did.

It would be after 1:00 A.M. when I would catch the train home from the City to Brooklyn, they ran about once every hour late nights. If I missed it, I would have to wait another hour before the next one came, and I would already be so tired that I didn't want to wait further. It didn't matter though I had to do what I had to do to survive. It wasn't so bad travelling on the subway in those days or walking the streets by yourself. As the times changed, people changed also. Things deteriorated eventually; the drug epidemic took over every aspect of many lives. The Republican President Ronald Reagan was linked to the origins of crack cocaine in California to the contras, a guerrilla force backed by the Reagan Administration that attacked Nicaragua's Sandinista government in the 1980s according to an article the National Security Archive, at the George Washington University. (The Contras, Cocaine, and Covert Operations https://nsarchive2.gwu.edu/NSAEBB/NSAEBB2/index.html)

They decided to flood the poor neighborhoods with drugs that destroyed countless lives in American cities throughout the country. The detrimental effects are still being felt today in many areas which never had a problem previously.

I had been working for a few months at Sbarro's doing the right thing. It had been a long time since I had sex and felt a need to get a little bit. I tried to hook up with some of the girls in my circle, but they were not feeling me like that I supposed. I went out looking for someone to fill my needs. There was a grocery store around the corner from my house and I went to have a beer. After I drank the one, I started on the next; it felt like my addiction calling me to get high all over, so I ended up buying some crack from a spot and took my first blast. It was just enough to get me started to the races; after the initial one I wanted more until I finished all my money. I never thought about all I accomplished or the things I acquired. My brother-in-law was a dealer, so I asked him if he had anything, he sold me enough to cook up a nice chunk. When I cooked it up, I added some nitroglycerin tablets to it; I called myself experimenting with no real knowledge of what I was doing.

I went out and found a girl who wanted to get high for sex; this was a pattern I developed since the early days. We went back to my house with my dad and sister there. I started getting high in my room with the crackhead then she started acting up. After I had given her something to smoke, she didn't want to do anything, just stood around looking at me waiting for me to give her more. I let her out and my dad locked the doors and told me to stay in the house, he was concerned. I tried to listen to him, but my mind kept spinning; it was saying that I should try to get more stuff. My heart was racing from the nitroglycerin tabs mixed with the coke. After a while I became frustrated more by the minute. Finally, I spoke to my father, telling him to give me my money I asked him to hold for me earlier, but he refused. After several attempts to get my cash, I got fed up and grabbed a 22.-cal pistol I sold him one day that was under his bed. I went to my room and grabbed a brand-new white sweatsuit I had bought a couple of weeks earlier. I went to the front room and pushed on a window until it gave way. I managed to squeeze through it and went in front of the building, the broken window had taken on the shape of my silhouette; there was a car running so I just hopped in and began to drive. I slammed the door not even knowing whose car it was. I floored it till I got to the corner, then I turned the wheel and sped toward the next street, made a left and hit a dumpster. The bumper locked on it, and I became frantic. Thrusting the car backwards then forwards and in reverse a few times till it became free. I started the wrong way down a side street; I saw a cop car coming straight my way; thought they were coming after me, so I floored it. My car picked up speed, moving faster towards having a head on. As I looked way down the line of sight the cop car turned off, so I slowed the vehicle down and took it to the crack spot on Palmetto Ave, a few blocks from my house. I left the car still running, I asked one of the crack heads to help me shut it off. When I got there, I tried to sell the sweatsuit, but they were broke and didn't want to give me a fair price, so I went to the hotel on the corner. There was a guy there he gave me about twenty dollars for the stuff.

When I finished smoking, I called my dad, and he was flabbergasted. I told myself I would never let somebody hold my money again. We obviously didn't agree completely. The money he had was mine, I worked for it, but he felt the need to control me like a little boy. Then to top it all off he called my Parole Officer and told him what had happened. The P.O. left a message for me to call him. When things calmed down, I called, and he told me to come in. I felt so awful going back to the Facility not knowing what was going to happen. I tried to tie a tube of water down in my groin area to squirt it out when I got there. As I was fumbling with the device inside the facility the officer noticed it and took me into custody. I couldn't believe it, just a few minutes ago I was a free man.

They took me up to the seventh floor, Cook's County. They had named the unit after this officer who was in charge, CO Cook. When I arrived, they placed me in a small bull pen till they were ready to process me. The processing was short, then the escort happened to come quickly. There were several double bunk beds stacked across the floor. Altogether there must have been enough room for twenty inmates. Everyone on this floor had screwed up and was waiting to go back up top. No one liked the isolation of those prison camps being far away from home, away from their loved ones. The women from the city always looked so much better and lovelier in comparison to the women by the prisons. The truth is after being locked up for a while they all begin to look a little better, somewhat inviting. Just to hear a women's voice or standing close by one can get you excited, even if they have the appearance of a buffalo butt, or a Gila monster. A whole lot of strange things happen when you are frozen in time. The life that we left behind becomes so important now, even if there's nothing we can do to get it back.

I went in the room where Sergeant Cook assigned me, the guys laying in their beds followed me with their eyes. After a few minutes they started giving me the third degree; they wanted to know what I had done to become a member of the group. I told them the story of me drinking beer and smoking crack, they laughed. One of them asked me how many I did, I said about fourteen. After that night they started calling me fourteen cracks, which I didn't mind so much. It was just another way for us to have some fun. It was easier to think of things that made me happier than to allow the reality of my situation to bog me down. Just like a routine when I went to any facility, the initial reckoning of being there wore off, then I fell in place finding my niche. In this case I realized I was going back upstate where I had just left not too long ago, also contemplating the reasons that led me back.

There were no fancy meals for breakfast, but hardly anything extra, most of the time lacking a favorable taste. Nothing was the same as a dark doomsday cloud lingered over my head, the only thing I thought about was where I was going to be sent to. I was given a ticket, or infraction for my violation, this was the prelude to my hearing held by the deputy superintendent. When they had the hearing, I was found guilty of getting a dirty urine, which was one of the worst things to be charged with. Three weeks later I was on the bus heading towards Sing Sing. When I initially arrived, I was amazed by the way prisoners spoke freely and even challenged the officers when they felt they were being disrespected. The mentality was having life or massive amounts of time behind them, they didn't mind at all for the little freedoms they enjoyed. When I went into the mess hall and asked for food, the line workers gave me as much as I wanted usually within reason. That means I packed on the rice, potatoes, and bread. Very rarely did I go to bed hungry while I stayed in Sing Sing. The commissary was also quite extensive for the taste of inmates who been down so long that it was wise to accommodate them however they could. One of the worst things I remember was the brownish colored drinking water; it was horrible, not like the clean crisp New York City tap, eventually I got used to the different taste.

Almost two months after being in Sing Sing, I was moved to the medium camp next door to it called Tai-Pan. This was a step down security-wise, but it had more freedoms. Inside Tai-Pan the facility gave us access to stovetops with ovens. The commissary was better and most of all we were able to peer through the fence to see the Hudson River just over the horizon. There were seagulls and pigeons that hung around waiting for the inmates to come by from the mess hall with bread to feed them. Sometimes I gave them a couple of slices, but the facility didn't like us doing that. The birds would shit all over the place. The food was good too; it seems as though it could have been the same as food from the other jails and prisons, but it tasted better when the inmates weren't always stressed out. Moving from a maximum prison always having to watch your back, to a medium where it was a bit laxer helps an inmate do an easier bid. I had to go to flooring classes back at Sing Sing from Tai-Pan; all the classes were great as well as the instructors. They always treated us with respect and kindness. After leaving my classes I would go back to my bunk, wind down and cook some food. I learned some of the other guy's techniques cooking the perfect red rice with *pulpo* (octopus), also other special dishes.

Before I knew it, time had passed; I finished my violation and was placed back on parole. One morning they packed me up to get on the bus to go to Edgecombe Correctional Facility, another Work Release Camp. This one was up by the Hamilton Heights area. This community was stationed right by the prison. I was able to observe other people through their windows and thought to myself what it would be like to be in their lives. When I used to have dreams, while I was younger; I imagined myself as a spirit visiting people, flying in their windows observing them or just walking around in their apartments. It was okay sometimes but, at other times it would turn scary, like into a nightmare. Big dogs might be running after me biting, barking, snarling, vicious or another type of frightening creature threatening my safety. I would often dream of many different things in this unusual but uncanny way when I was younger, but as the years passed me by my dreams became farther and few in between. As the leaves fall from the trees so did my magical dreams seem to disappear. They gave me a vigor, a zest for adventure, a freedom that undulated creative juices unparalleled in other phases of my life.

As always, I hung around the kitchens a natural habit; I remember working in most of them when I was allowed to, it helped the time go and kept my belly full especially when I didn't have money to buy my own commissary. While most guys had family or girlfriends who would send them money, my family didn't really subscribe to that magazine, if I were locked up, I was on my own apart from my big brother Fred. He served as a military officer as an MP, and he was more empathetic in this area. It was a kind of blur from the time I arrived at Edgecombe Facility, but one day they let me out. This was an unfamiliar territory for me in Washington Heights wandering about with many shady looking characters lurching closely. I had a little over a hundred dollars when I left that morning; everything was fine till I reached a stop on the train which became the nexus for my next relapse. Some voice reverberated in my nimble brain to get off the train and see if there was a place to score. It was around Spanish Harlem by 125th Street that this nightmare began. After I took the first pull off the pipe my dick started acting up; I thought I wanted to fuck, but that rarely happened when I got high. First I take the hit, then the hit takes me, usually off to a bad place when the get high ended. I had to wonder how I managed to stay alive for so many years using drugs and alcohol, and just for the record, in the rooms of Narcotics Anonymous alcohol is considered a drug also.

After a couple of months on the street the Division of Parole caught up to me and served me with an abscondence violation. I couldn't believe how I looked when they finally brought me in. I was dirty, smelly, and broke; I had the jackass look on my face and sorry as shit. I was glad I didn't catch an added charge on top of the violation, which would have been devastating. When it was all said and done, the worst thing they told me was that I would never be eligible for Work Release again. To me that meant something that I couldn't ever be trusted again in that capacity.

A few months later, I was on a bus going back to the city; the bus slowly crossed the terrain into the lanes of the bridge. The smog filled air left a thick dark cloud suspended over the city, as I came closer to my destination: the Port Authority bus station. I started hearing voices in my head telling me to get high. I fought them back while I tried to reason with myself as to why I shouldn't go back down that road. For a good ten minutes I struggled with the thought and finally the pressure became so great that I went into the toilet on the bus and vomited. I felt a little relief from the demon until I got to my sister's house. When I arrived, I greeted my sister, hugged, and kissed my mother who was now staying with her and went to the bathroom. Then I asked my brother, who had something, if he could go and cop for me. He didn't mind but I felt he didn't want to go; that he wanted me to stay straight.

When it was finished, I had borrowed money from my mother that night and I was embarrassed at my actions. I had left some of my possessions in a lockbox at the Port Authority, so I went to retrieve them and sold a few that day when I picked them up to get some cash. There were some porcelain pieces that I made in the arts and crafts shop; I laid them on the ground and waited for people to make me an offer. When I went home, I had her money, placed it in her hand and she was happy. Happy that I was home, but not happy to see me still getting high. I never thought about the pain I was causing her to see me in this state. What I noticed was how she didn't have that same happiness she felt about me years ago. She was no longer so immensely proud of me and what I had become. Her feelings were different for me now, and I was oblivious to the precious feelings of her heart. She saw me go from sugar to shit, but never did she fix her mouth to tell me how miserably disappointed she had been lately, always the eternal introvert.

During the nineteen eighties, cocaine moved from the freebase to crack, a much cheaper form to keep the funds flowing into the pockets of the so-called dealers. These guys were just peons slaving for the kingpins such as Pablo Escobar and the Ochoa's from Columbia, and people of color who amassed enormous wealth by saturating the poorest communities of American cities with their poison. Many years of destruction has taken its toll on generations of many black people and others. The term *crack babies* were initially coined for the victims of the children of crack addicts. The lives of so many children became a living hell for them to try and coexist with their parents. Hardly any regular daily normalcy, feeding, cleaning, or nurturing the needs of individuals. Dishes piled to the ceiling, roaches and rats running ramped, floors strewn with debris and filth to the highest levels. Funds for regular normal needs was a scarcity in most crack-plagued households. Most of them lacked food or a warm family to greet children when they arrived from school. It was often better running away from home, bonding with strangers in gangs or with others who dealt drugs to navigate the harsh reality of extreme poverty. The Republicans, under the direction of Ronald Reagan, sought to gain funds for the Contras, in a war that Congress wouldn't fund, so they decided to flood their dope in our communities which wreaked havoc and destroyed many households in our nation.

I never think about the life I had before I started using drugs, it was so refreshing and full of excitement; it's all gone now but on the journey back to my reality, I look better every day, one day at a time. After engaging hard-core addiction, always in and out of my house, being up all night, after night, day after day, year after year, things didn't seem so bleak, it was though, I just couldn't see it; I didn't know how screwed up I was. As time moved on my cravings increased more and more when I got high I became a feign. My brother let me use his Reel-to-Reel tape player, so one day being so thirsty, I asked him if I could sell it; he told me sure, just get enough for it or something similar. My sister Bunny heard about what I wanted to do and decided to intervene; she thought it best to hide it from me so I couldn't sell it. I became so infuriated that I later took some stuff of hers, and other things around the house. I had never taken anything or stolen from people before this time. She had a silverware set from her son's deceased father which I sold, also I took some VHS tapes my brother brought with him from being in the service. I felt so sorry about it later when there was absolutely nothing I could do about it. One of the many things I regretted through the years of my unforgettable addiction. I know I stole from my own house, something that never sat well with me. I found out if I asked people, mostly strangers I could get enough to supply my habit, I then became a beggar, a habit I learned from the Ansar Community on Bushwick Ave, they were a radical Muslim sect. Sometimes I was able to borrow a few dollars from my mom or other people in my house, but this became worn down soon enough. They got tired of me asking for money to get high. Quite often people gave me their ass to kiss, told me to fuck off because they were fed up.

Sometime after on this dreary night I somehow managed to get hold of my mother's purse. She had just gotten her check and most of her money was there. I took it and went over to my dad's house and when I looked at the money, I didn't realize it or want to spend it all, so I told my dad what I had done. Then told him I only wanted to spend ten dollars of the six hundred plus dollars. I asked him to hold the rest of the money, I was going to put it back when I went home later that morning. So, he held it for me as I went out to get a dime of crack. I did it then came back to the house and after a while I fell asleep. That morning he took me home and I went in the door then I snuck back into the closet where she had it and placed the cash back in the spot where I took it from. Don't think she ever knew it was missing. After that I wanted to go away to get some help. I told her about me going to a program and she was so happy for me. She gave me a few dollars to get there and some extra to buy whatever. Later the next day I got on the train headed for the program; I passed Bushwick into Williamsburg on the train I thought about getting high again and soon got off. I landed up by Lorimer or Marcy Ave, searching for some get high. At this point I no longer held on to that thing called pride; I could see how I disappointed my dear, kind, loving mother. One of the things I suffered from was low self-esteem. I could often hear how others said condescending things to me, about me, how the words of others played a part in my demeanor. Those words also affected my mother's image of me.

"Don't let them say those things to you, Johnnie."

She would often take up my battle, how I remember she told me to stand up for myself whenever I was being ridiculed.

I don't want to use that as an excuse, but I heard their voices in my head while I was doing what I was doing.

A day later I made it back home with the jackass look on my face; my mom was wondering what happened, why I didn't follow through. I told her the truth about me getting side-tracked, how I got off the train and the unforgettable look on her face when I told her. It was one of loathing, despair, and grief; I hated wearing my skin on that day, I knew I had crossed over into something most repulsive coupled with disdain. All I could do was get out of her face. She thought of how she could have borne a son so unlikely in her womb. Whatever she may have been feeling, she never let me know her thoughts; she just looked at me momentarily, then moving on committed to her diurnal affairs.

My sister had friends who were hustlers, money men that chased paper even while in their dreams. Some of them came by and we made acquaintances. At some point they had this powerful heroin that would make you go in a dope feign nod; it was called C.O.D. which stood for (Cash On Delivery) So, they had formed a crew and gave work to a couple of the guys around my house to make some money. They also asked me to work for them. My sister's friend was named Kareem, and he looked out for me. He knew I was fucked up and gave me an opportunity to make money selling crack by his house in Flatbush. I was fine with that because it was easy. Also, Kareem was very nice to me; the first day I went by his house he took me in, fed me then tended to any of my needs. The next morning, he took me out and told me to stay close to a spot he had chosen, where his clientele would come to cop. He gave me $110 dollars of product at a time. $100 was his and the $10 was for me.

At first it was a little slow, then it picked up. On a good day I stayed high having enough to buy beers and have a little extra. His people began to know who I was and looked forward to seeing me. Some of the ladies wanted to have sex with me if I gave them some, I did. When the shop was closing, as they had made their quota, they shut down the operation and gave me some pay. That was mostly in crack and a few dollars. They would also take me home and tell me to be ready the next day. This was better than begging. I had fun making money with these guys for a while, until I screwed up. I messed up a package and the boss, Toughie took a heavy pipe or stick and whacked me once on my arm to let me know it was not a joke. I didn't like that, but I handled it, took it like a man. I stayed out there in Flatbush for a few months I guess, then it was time to leave. I eventually went back to my neighborhood then started selling their dope downstairs in my sister's building. Two brothers living with their mother downstairs (Sly and Shugg), were the initial ones Toughy and Kareem gave their dope to sell for them. The money started rolling in, the dopeheads found out it was there, and it immediately became popular. They had to have it; it was that dope from way back in the old days when it started, probably back in the sixties. I took a sniff here and there not knowing what to expect, I started nodding after a few tries, then I stopped doing it so I wouldn't get hooked. The dope feigns told me to watch out for a chipper, the beginnings of a dope habit as it gets a grip on you. After a little while on the scene I was selling the dope for them too. I would get a ten spot off a hundred, that was enough to supply my crack habit for the meantime.

It was cool out on this summer night, the wind blowing ever so gently as I hung down in the hole waiting for customers. I finished one batch and had the cash on me with the rest of the stash. It was getting late, and I wanted to smoke. I took a hit and went outside with five bundles of their dope. My intention was to sell it but the get high change my plans; before I knew it, I was off to the races. I smoked up all the money and when I finished all the dope was gone too. I remember so clearly when I got on the bus and took a sniff, I couldn't keep my eyes open. I was falling asleep from the dope; it was strong.

I managed to go by an area where a lot of people used it, by Knickerbocker and Troutman in the Bushwick part of town. When I got there, I gave out a few samples to try and get some money to buy some crack. That didn't go so well, most of the people were crying broke wanting to freeload off my dumb ass. This one dope addict tried to make a deal with me; he was going to get some coke and share it with me for some of the dope. He took me to a place long and far away from where I met him, there I waited till he finished his business and then we went back to the area we came from. I stayed there for a while listening to the songs and dances of the regulars in the neighborhood, then when I ran out of stuff everybody else was gone too.

I walked the streets wondering how I managed to get myself in this screwed up position again. I walked and walked till I started asking people for change, this was a real kick in the head, I felt like such a loser. I walked till I got to Evergreen and Linden by a grocery store. I walked in and asked one of the guys to help me to get a beer. He looked at me like he couldn't believe what he was seeing, a big guy nice and handsome asking people for change like a bum off the street. He had a talk with me and asked me if I was willing to put in some work for some real money. He wanted me to shoot somebody, commit a crime. I thought about it and spoke confidently to him about the job. At first, I was willing to get involved with his offer. He told me I should be more confident when I approached people and be more aggressive, demanding what I wanted. The time passed while in his company with many people that knew him, they gave him the utmost respect. He bought me beers and finally gave me a twenty to get high with, I was supposed to meet him the next day by the store. I went away and thought about what I was going to do, it just didn't sit well with me. I wasn't a real killer, at least not then. When the next day came, I found myself on the Coney Island beach looking at the waves wondering where my feet were going to take me next. I was just off and wandering aimlessly through life with no meaning or purpose.

As the cool air blew softly over the salty sandy beach I reached in my pockets and realized that I was dead broke, not even two nickels to rub together. How many times had I come down this road; being at the end of a binder impecuniously looking in the mirror with the Jackass look on my face. W-T-F am I doing this precarious position? Isn't there anything more that my life has to offer besides being a broke dick dog? How am I going to recover from this mess? It seemed like the story was always the same ole' one, I get some drugs, get high, then wind up somewhere without enough cash to buy a fifty-cent soda. Poor me. Anyway, I mustered enough courage to go back to my sister's house, hoping I wouldn't have to face the music. I walked down the lightly filth strewn beach to the Coney

Island station and hopped the turn-style. I waited for the train a couple of minutes and boarded it when the doors opened. I looked a bit funky, so I was happy to get a seat to myself. The other people that got on didn't really notice me much. I was so tired that I rode past the stop having fell asleep.

When I woke up, I was all the way uptown by the Bronx. I road it back again and the same thing happened, I couldn't stay awake. When I finally reached my sister's house, I found out that my mother was in the hospital. I was a bit disoriented, but I went to see her in Saint Mary's Hospital on Franklin Ave. I went into the lobby and asked the clerk if they could tell me where she was placed. I was directed to the ICU. At first the gravity of the situation was not clear, so I just haphazardly waltzed into the ICU. There she was on a nice clean bed propped up high with my younger sister by her side. They were speaking softly to each other, then my sister announced to her that I was also there. My mother looked up at me as if she was so happy to see me. I hugged her with joy that only we shared for each other. I was awfully glad to see her but not in the condition I was in; my clothes were a bit dirty, my hair unkempt and I reeked of despair and destitution.

She looked at me and spoke, "Johnnie, I know you been out there in those streets, and you been getting high, running around doing who knows what. I wish I could make the person who invented that crack stuff a special place to burn in hell. I would punish them so severely that they would wish they were never born. I can't take the taste from your mouth; I can't fight that battle for you. I've giving you everything I could. I truly hope you get off that stuff Johnnie, it ain't doing nothing but destroying you. You are my son and I love you; it hurts me so much to see you like this. I know it's hard, but you can do it."

I looked at her knowing everything she said was true, I knew I had been a big disappointment to her since I fell from my previous station in life. How she used to brag about me to her group of friends when I was working as a messenger. I was only a source of embarrassment to her now. How much damage have I done to her precious, loving heart? I was so far gone that I'd been oblivious to all the hurt I caused her. My actions were killing her inside, while I didn't know all her feelings. I never thought about all the pain I've been causing my mother. I stayed for a while listening to her and my sister chit chat, staying by their side to support them. Time passed until we had to go, the nurse informed us that the visit was over. I held my mother and kissed her goodnight while somewhere in my heart I said to myself that I was going to straighten up and turn a new leaf, get a new lease on life. I walked into the dark cool air longing for a place to rest my head, somewhere safe and warm.

I stayed out in the streets all that day running after the drugs getting high. When it was dark again and I was lonely, I thought of seeing my mother before visiting hours was over, so I made my way back to the hospital. I had my crack-pipe on me, and I made it to the ICU; outside was a nurse sought of standing in my way when I approached.

"Hello, I'm here to see my mother, Mrs. Davis." Not saying anything at first, just looking at my face she spoke.

"Would you come over here, and take a seat?"

"For what? what's wrong? Is my mother dead?"

"Yes, she passed this morning."

Anything after that was a blur, I went to the restroom and thought I'd hit the pipe, but I didn't feel anything. I had lost all my feelings inside, and I just started walking, traveling till I came to Williamsburg. I bought a few beers and was trying to make some sense of what had just happened. I drank the beers, then thought about all the wonderful things my mother had done for me in my life. The thought kept reverberating in my head, my mother's gone. No more walks to the park, no kissing my wounds after I was cut, telling me to be careful. On cold nights she won't be there to place a blanket over my cold shivering body. No one to bring an apple or orange to after a long journey. All the little things I used to do mean so little now, having no one to do them for. How many things do people in the world long for? Perhaps a house to live in, a car that they really like, a relationship with a wonderful person. All the things people long for mean nothing to me; the only thing I want any more is to see the smile on my mother's face, knowing she is proud of me, knowing she is happy I'm her son. At that moment I buckled over and started crying uncontrollably. I was wailing with intense grief, feeling and all the anxiety of my selfish actions from the time I started getting high. All the bad experiences which I thought were good when I was doing them, didn't equal one moment of joy I felt when I was close to my dear sweet mother.

"Oh God what have I done?" I cried, but there was no one there to answer me. I put my face in my lap and continued.

The next day I sought the comfort of my siblings and made my way towards my sister's house. When I got there, we were all in a sad state, nobody said or did anything to disrupt the mood. Even the guys that I took the product from were not pressing me for the payment for the drugs I had taken. It was quite possible that it may have been a contributing factor in my mom's death. All I know, it was water under the bridge now.

Many people came through giving their condolences and paying their respect. For me it was as if I was a fish out of water; I stood around not getting high, not being used to being around people without the use of a crutch, a vehicle to alter my state of mind. I tried my best to stay sober for as long as I could but eventually, I was led right back to the get high well. I hated the fact that I had so much in life previously and was now impecuniously hanging on other people's purse-strings. I didn't have a job, clothes, car, women, house or enough to buy a Happy Meal. Many mornings I woke up dead broke, and this was a real problem. Many people got high but maintained their lifestyle to some degree. For me it was all just a waste of time, nothing stayed my way, the way I wanted them to be, only for a night or a day, or part of a day. People only used me for my cash, and then when the party was over, they were gone too. I led myself to believe that people cared about me; that they were hanging around me because they genuinely liked me for the person I was. After many years of the hard facts that I was not what I thought I was to people, I learned to readjust my way of thinking. I accepted the fact that many people didn't like me or have a desire to be in my life. So, I lived, and I learned. Now my days are filled with doing positive things for me and helping others when I can, just if it doesn't affect me. It was a tragic day for all my siblings, the day our mother passed, we all wished we had done better by her. I know I can't take back the past, but if I can help someone else benefit from my experiences, it will be the least I can do. The one thing I want to pass on to others is that if you have a mother, and she is still alive; make her know how much you love her and care for her. Try hard to be a good person, one that will honor her when she is no longer around, because when she's gone you can't make up for the things you wished you had done for her.

I managed to find myself by my dad's house again, the latest events were still fresh in my mind. I stayed there with him, and he was kind of reluctant to have me there, maybe the thought of me stealing things made him keep his distance. I was there, but not all the way in my heart and mind, the drugs were still eating at me. He sent me to the store for something, when I got back, he asked me to go to the store again. This happened about three or four times, and when I went out the last time, I took a portion of the money to buy some crack, I figured I could pan-handle the money back in no time and go back to the house. That was the last time I saw my father alive. I loved my dad as much as my mother, but I fucked up and let them both down.

This time I walked the streets for hours, then days until I made it to the city. There was a place by West 8th Street in the Path train station where I often slept at night when it was cold outside. Each night the Volunteers of America would come by with police escorts and ask if I wanted to go to the shelter. Most of the time I told them no, until they told me about all that I could do there. They said I could take a shower, get some fresh clothes to put on, and that was my ticket. They sold me the idea, so I went with them. While there one night I found enough courage to call my dad. I told him I was sorry, I was more than sorry though, leaving under my circumstances left me in shambles. The only thing I could do was to continue to try and get high. I could smoke all day and night but not feel what I was looking for. The connectivity with people was gone, I had lost my sense of humanity. I felt like a bungling, blithering idiot. I lost my mother on February 3rd the previous year, and my dad died on the same day one year later.

It happened, I managed to get myself locked up again. It was not funny, but I would get hungry during the day and night at Wards Island, the shelter where I was staying. In the mornings I would go out and walk across the pedestrian bridge over the East River and walk around El Barrio (Spanish Harlem). There I would find ways to get high and hang out on the streets until it was time to be back in the shelter. Somehow, I met some guys that was selling crack and they put me on. I would sell a few, then smoke a few, it was good for me for a short while. No sooner than I sold my third pack I got busted. I went to jail and the real drug dealer went home to his family. When I went to court, I had to cop out or face a lengthier prison sentence for going to trial. The cards were stacked against me, the courts were rigged to put the users in prison and let the dealers go. That was the American way.

While I was away in jail my dad died, and I felt a great remorse. The two most influential people in my younger life were now gone forever. With my dad, the memories of him trying to teach me things, taking me with him, consoling him when he thought about what happened to his family. How he stayed bitter for many years after he and my mother separated. I don't think he wanted that, but he tried to manage being alone until I came. Night after night in that big house with no one to care for him, no one to talk to and share his thoughts with. His only friend was a bottle of Johnnie Walker; that was until I came to stay with him. Then I left him and now he was gone too.

The prison let me go to the funeral where my family came to pay their last respects. My dad wasn't always an easy person to get along with, he didn't always fit in the most likable category, but he was himself, he was honest to his feelings, and I loved him for the person he was. I wished many times I wouldn't have walked off with his money that day when I went to the store for him, for the last time. There are many things in life that I regret doing, I try hard not to do them again once I learned from my mistakes. Nothing says that all learning would be fun or easy, but it sure is fun not to bring yourself to hurt or ruins.

When the funeral was finished, I went back to the prison and thought about my experiences. How I was so fortunate not to be back on the streets smoking crack and doing things that could place me in jeopardy. There were times I took great chances with my life to find a means to get high. One day while I was riding on the back of a truck to see if I could enter it from the back when it stopped at the light. I got on the truck, and it seemed to never slow down and at one point I had to get off, so when it slowed down just enough, I took a chance and jumped off. I was sliding and tumbling in the street, bruised up and scraped from the fall when I finally managed to break free from the ride to hell. I stole things many times from trucks like that, which I truly regret today, this was my way of maintaining my habit. I always worked alone though, after my first encounter with other black guys. I didn't like robbing people at all, I wasn't brought up that way; it wasn't until my sister had stolen from me that I developed that bad habit of stealing; however, it was still wrong.

At night in my cell or cubicle, I would think of where I was in life, how I had little to show for all my experiences: no wife, children, house, cars, material wealth, just a big, long history for getting high. What an awful pity I thought, living all my years to waltz right into a poverty-stricken stature, suffering from the likes of bums and shiftless lay abouts. I know I could aspire to be more if I apply myself, I must break free of this rut.

The facility where I was staying was called Mount McGregor. It was perched high on a mountain, and they called it Magic Mountain. The theory was if you invested much stock into the treatment program that you will be free from drug addiction. As brothers went through the program, I noticed the changes in their behavior. They may lie a little less, or not steal something that they normally would have, whatever it was, it seemed to be working. Those subtle differences told whether a person was serious about their recovery. The sky didn't open wide, and Jesus didn't come floating down on a magic rug sprinkling fairy dust creating miracles over the complex, but I felt something like magic over time.

Before I was to be released, I tried to get paroled to Texas by my brother's place, but the New York State Division of Parole wouldn't allow me to go to another state, they wanted to keep me here in the Big Dirty, Rotten Apple. It wasn't always the Big Dirty, Rotten Apple, there was a time when people here could live a good life and flourish in New York City. Life was so much better on a grander scale then. People did or could leave their doors open if they wanted to, that was before however many years ago. They were different as the years passed by and so did the quality of the residents. It had something to do with the massive influx of immigrants that didn't live by rules in their country, who moved here and disregarded the laws we had in place; then started living like they did back in their old countries. It's not easy to pinpoint any definite cause, it just happened through the ages; nowadays if a person gets in a car accident, the driver takes off immediately, whereas years ago the driver would have stayed on scene, to make sure the person they hit was okay, that's just one Example. Also, by no means do I blame our society's ills on immigrants either; we all have a hand in making it either better or worse.

My dad left his house without a will, so that meant that we all had a share in the inheritance (my siblings and I). My brother sent me some papers to sign while I was locked away and he sent me some of the inheritance money. He didn't send all of it, so I had to get the rest of my inheritance from him when I got out of prison. I had to deduct the amount he owed from the rent I paid. I remember wanting one of his classic cars, he had two Buick Electric 225's and other things; but when you are away, there's very little you can do to get a fair share of anything. Most of the things didn't really matter to me anyway. The most important things he left me were not material, they were a sense of humanity. He had a way with life, a style of his own. He often spoke about how he was a God-fearing man, and that is the most important lesson that he taught me was to be God fearing. Even though he did wrong at times, he knew he did, or was doing wrong at the time, but he didn't stop himself. Many of us struggle with the same plight, knowing we are doing wrong but don't prevent ourselves from the continuance of the act. He was always praying to God in the best way he knew how. Sometimes in the mist of his struggles he would cry uncontrollably, and I would hold him close to me and comfort him. Some people think that men should not cry or be emotional, but I feel if a person does, they are being honest with their feelings. My parents have taught me to fear God and ask for his forgiveness and guidance; so far it has brought me through many years.

Since my brother now owned the house, I had to stay there to recoup some of my inheritance money. After getting situated I started going to the city buying clothes to sell on the streets. My pockets began to get fat from that hustle, I started with a few items, then evolved to many different things which increased my revenue. There were others who did the same thing I did, but they didn't stick with it. I bought a nice Trek bike from a friend that helped me to cover much more ground. I went through a few neighborhoods with my goods, but I was aware that it carried a level of risk. Some guys were jealous and always liked the easy way out of everything, they wanted to rob and steal from me, but I didn't have time for those dumb childish games. I felt the best remedy for those slackers is a good knot upside their heads. It seems no matter where you go in life there's always somebody trying to find a way to disrupt your flow. If they can find an angle to make a quick dollar, there's always a Jackass trying to find a way to get yours, instead of getting their own.

After a few months of good sales and having a steady positive cash flow, I started looking for girls to have sex with. I found them in unusual places and offered them cash for sex. Sometimes I was successful, and other times not. After spending so much time locked up, I wanted to have sex with a lady nice and hot, with some snapback; a woman that wanted to be loved and cared for. The only problem was I didn't want to spend the rest of my life trying to achieve this goal. Let me get my nuts out the sand first, then all the rest of the rigmarole. Every day I saw more beautiful woman that were available, but just not for me. Some of them were so stuck up in the air that to talk to them would have only been a waste of time. In this case I wish there were an uncomplicated way out. I was never trying to prove a point, I just enjoyed them, having good sex. The more I do it the better I wish I were at it. I would watch porn movies to get pointers and learn better techniques. Sometimes I think I was a good lay, but there was a whole lot I didn't know, a lot I didn't do.

My friend Brandy was cute, brown-skinned with a pleasant personality. I saw her one day coming up my block and we hit it off. I started screwing her for a few dollars at a time, maybe $15 or $20. It must have come to a point that the amount I was giving her wasn't sufficient, she stopped coming by. For whatever the reason I hoped to find more like her. I wanted more than they were willing to give. After chasing the pussy for a while that wasn't enough, so I started using drugs and alcohol again to fill the void, I guess. Before I knew it, I was going full throttle in get high mode. Nobody that knew me could understand why I chose to go back down that road again and again. At the end of this run, my brother put all my possessions out on the street without notice and I had nowhere to take them. There was this two-bit drug dealer that had a little vestibule by a storefront that let me place my possessions there. As time went by, he found a reason to jerk me, I was sweet on his daughter who noticed me watching her. Now I was homeless again, I hated the thought that I could do good for so many people and when I needed help, they were not around, not available to help me. Over, and over time after time this was the pattern. I learned to stay to myself more and more, or at least I tried to. No matter how it happened though these people always seem to find a way to weasel their way into my life; I would be doing great without their presence, the moment they enter in my life, shit starts going awry for the worse I had to learn that to move forward in the direction I wanted to go. Year after year I was always having to start over, usually for the dumbest reasons, perhaps I wasn't aggressive enough; but when I stayed to myself, I always managed to get to the goals that I was aiming for.

My older brother worked hard to become a drug counselor at a program, and he convinced me to go into treatment. I left with the intention of getting clean and staying off drugs, all the hoopla, bells and whistles sounded so fantastic. I arrived at the Renaissance Project on a weekday, way up in the boon docks, in a place called Ellenville, up-state New York. They would wake us up about 5:30

A.M. to get ready for breakfast. It must have been about 180 people in the whole compound, men, and women. We had to get medicated, then eat breakfast before the morning meeting, which was about 8:00 A.M. We would stand around and listen to the structure preach to us then go about doing our numerous chores. I came to the morning meetings still half sleep hoping they were over before they began. It felt like they were trying to ram the program down our throats, or to force us to believe in their crackpot doctrine will cure us and save us from eternal damnation. Like most twelve step programs, they say it works if you work it. I guess I never worked it because it never worked for me. Regardless I tried to live by the rules and hung in there even when others through shit in the game. Some of the residents just flat out lied on me about doing things I obviously didn't do. This was one of the things that irked me so much about being there, having to live among people that didn't like me for whatever reason, and yet they used their limited power to cause more chaos in my torn and tattered life. These were some of the most unscrupulous miscreants that deserved a good thrashing, also probably would never find true inner peace. At times my skin would crawl just knowing they were near; perhaps these words are a bit strong, I don't want to seem un-compassionate.

Some of the girls started looking better after a while; they shared their stories which made me look at them sometimes more, sometimes less. I met Maureen Owens there who was a real looker. She was light skinned and had a nice fat round booty; her words were soft, and she always remained reserved. No matter how much I fancied her, the cards was just not having it. Everywhere I went in life, I always lost good love connections, but I never gave up trying to find them. Sometimes I feel like what's the use; I'm older now and don't want to take more chances at losing, that's the worst thing in the world for me. I can see if I was a bad guy or someone who never means any good to these women, but I'm not that guy. I just feel like treating them like shit, at least maybe they'll stick around and be there when I need them. That's how it seems to be for all the other guys who get the good girls. Who cares about living that kind of whack-a-doodle life anyway? For the most part I only wanted to get laid, get a piece of ass and keep it moving.

This program withheld most of the money from my checks; giving me only a small portion for cigarettes and walk-around-money (WAM), they held another portion for when I would be released. It was horrible the way these people bled us dry, keeping most of our cash for their own personal gain. Of course, they must get paid too, but it would have been nice to have a bigger slice of my own pie. One day I had gotten so fed up I just had to leave; I couldn't stomach the place any further. They allowed me to pack my clothes, then took me to the small-town bus stop. For my pockets after being there 5 months, I was only given approximately $184.00. What a shithole.

I headed back to the city to my family again; they didn't want me to come, but I had nowhere else to go. I started going to an out-patient program when I left. It was at Cumberland Hospital Clinic in the Fort Green section of Brooklyn. They wanted me to come from 8:30 A.M. to 3:00 P.M. 5 days a week: making meetings all day, then another one at night. This was a living hell; hearing people share their experience strength and hope repeatedly. I could never figure out the dynamics of other people's psychology; I grew weary from the journey, but I remained committed till the end. In the beginning when I went to the program, I tried to stay focused, not trying to get with some of the girls there, they call that thirteen-stepping in the rooms of Narcotics Anonymous; that's when a guy or girl hits on the newcomers that may be vulnerable. All sunk in, their little asses, skinny malnourished and very talkative; those are some of the characteristics that are first noticed in the newcomers. They always say that the newcomer is the most important person in the meeting because we can't keep what we have if we don't give it away. After they are there for a while, they begin to learn the lingo, speaking like a pro, like they got it all under their belts, cocky if you will. There are many stages in recovery that are noticeable when you work the program, your life changes miraculously, you become a different person, one that people can tolerate again and won't mind you being in their presence. Sometimes things don't come to fruition, especially if you don't change your attitude and behavior. They say that you are a dry drunk when you put down the drugs and alcohol and still behave the same as you did before.

I had a friend that would walk with me every morning to the program even though we could have taken the bus or train. We would be getting it in arriving at the program just in time for us to clock in. This also helped me stay in shape after so many years of doing just that, walking. I never thought about all the benefits until I stopped doing it. My nephew Tyquan always says, "If you don't use it, you'll lose it." This is something I totally agree with as I've gotten older, because now my body has many more aches and pains that I never imagined would be there. I have much respect for older people who have debilitating diseases that control their abilities to perform their diurnal rituals.

Some days after the program I would walk home or at least part of the way. Looking at the brownstone buildings in Fort Greene, passing the storefronts and businesses along the way, taking in the sights of many lovely ladies walking about carefree. Often the B54 bus would be crowded but I moved swiftly through the streets navigating effortlessly through traffic. There was always a variety of lovely women walking along the sidewalks on any given day. The most important part of any day was when I reached home. I had to cook for myself and make sure I took my medicine for diabetes, if not things could get much worse for me physically. Then after I had taken care of all my needs I would wind down and fall asleep.

Chapter II

NA Rock, Nostrand Ave, Bedford Stuyvesant Brooklyn. In the nineteen eighties, it was Wild and Raw, the people were different. Many of the brothers I knew were hustlers or trying to be one, others worked normal jobs building their lives and supporting them. Me myself, since having committed two felonies precluded me from certain jobs, also not having skills demanded that I upgrade them to be more marketable. Many days I wished I would have made better choices, done things different and lived a better life. The problem is that I can't relive the experience, nor turn back the hands of time, I can only move on and rebuild from today.

I was at my sister Bunny's house on Nostrand Ave. again, I want to thank my sister for putting up with me for so many years, I know I could have been overbearing, not because I wanted to be, it's just the way I was. As time went on, I changed a little day by day also taking a good look at myself and making sure that I'm not just settling for what life has to offer but actively putting an effort to live the way I want to while I can, using all the talents God bestowed on me to the best of my ability.

It's fun to learn something new as I did for most of my life, at times I may have considered myself an academician; I must prove that I'm able to do what I say I can. One of the lessons I learned is to stay out of jail. I don't do crime anymore unless it's necessary. I never liked being couped up with other men living in proximity; that's the kind of crap this system has in store for us. The laws have been unfairly distributed between the races, classes, or whatever demographic we fell into, as this society tries to correct the actions of the past, things start to feel like they're getting better. I don't hold the white people of today responsible for the actions of their ancestors—after all I'm part white—I only hold them responsible for what they do today. I've met many people that have benefited me in some way. I also hope I can make someone's life better if they allow me to.

After being in and out of so many jails and institutions, not doing anything productive at different periods in my life I wanted to do something different and meaningful, so I decided to go to college to become a radiological technician. I found out the New York City College of technology offered the course and it fit right into my schedule. The first day I went I was greeted by the staff, they explained to me some of the steps I needed to take so I took them. Then the next important thing I realized was the money part was real, it costs money to get into school and maintain that lifestyle. There were so many obstacles that prevented other students from graduating, and it was my objective to avoid them.

My classes were at night, about 6:30 P.M. It was summertime and there were a few young troublemakers who were only there just to past the time away. I knew it was a struggle for them and understood some of the things they did prevented them from completing the process. I went to two other colleges previously before going here. One was Marymount College in Harlem by 125th Street, which I would go there late afternoons and ride the train home usually within a reasonable time. The second one was TCI on 8th Ave. on 33rd Street in mid-town Manhattan. I did a lot I guess for a guy who started working at 14 years old. It was even before then, I worked at a butcher grocery store for a week at age 8. Also, at a Korean Vegetable Market on Broadway and Ralph Ave in Brooklyn at age 10.

In the beginning, the college classes were a little hard to get used to. The hardest part was to study after classes, being that I never developed an efficient study pattern I had to figure it out. All throughout high school I breezed through the material hardly devoting more time than needed to any subject. Once I arrived at college the playing field changed, and I had to acclimate. They placed me in a remedial math class. Once I was in there, I feel I had been cheated out of most of my education for the fact that the material I was learning, I hadn't learned already. It is a pity to have people teach you how to be dumb or obsolete. It was as if I had never taken a course in math for my entire life, I had to learn the math all over. While I and most of the other students were there to learn, there was a few slackers that disrupted the class with their simple-minded antics. They came to class to make jokes, fool around and smoke weed on their breaks. Some of them had parents that paid their tuition; the look they gave when they flunked was worth a lot. Regardless I only knew I had to achieve my goal, so I kept coming.

The young ladies were looking better every day, especially when I got a word in edgewise. Some of them wanted to give me a little rhythm, but I had to stay focused; also, I was too old for most of them. For me it was a horrible experience trying to hook up with them. I didn't have a motive to do it, but some of them were so good-looking and it was hard to contain myself at times. At some part of a day or night I woke up and realized that I'm only human, and the young ladies remained desirable regardless of my cohorts and their perception. Here I was flossing among the most precious cutie pies after being locked up far away in prison, just wanting to be in the company of such beautiful young women. The many nights I spent peering through the cell bars wanting to speak to one, thinking about it, wishing I had one of my own. How I hated hearing the stories of the other inmates telling me how they were going to do it differently when they got out, do it better. The end was they were waiting to sell more drugs and commit crimes all over again before they even left the prison. I absolutely didn't want to hear none of that. From day to day, I longed to get a letter, a package, money in my account or a visit, like the other prisoners were getting. I wondered what I had done so horrible to the people I knew to make them abandon me like they did. The pain and emotional stress stayed with me throughout the whole of my bids. I wasn't a killer or real gangster; I was just an average guy that got caught up in the game.

The transition was always up front, I knew from where I came and how much I appreciated my own company. The women here in the city had a smooth softness about themselves that looked good. The only women I saw while I was upstate were rough looking Correction Officers that had ways that were not so feminine, they were not my type.

The semesters lasted a few weeks, maybe twelve or so. I received my first grade for my remedial math class. I got an F which I couldn't believe. I needed to get a C or better, to get a passing grade to get into the program I selected, the radiological technician or (Rad-Tech) program. I was so pissed off when I had to repeat the course. The hard part was I really tried to pass the class. Very rarely have I set out to do something and not do it. I was placed on academic probation and didn't want people to think I was not able to do the work. I immediately started looking for more ways to learn the material. Some of the other students made suggestions, but the most effective was to go to tutoring. So, every day when I finished class I went there.

There were a few tutors that helped with different levels of the math. Many of the young people took a strong dislike towards me; perhaps I was too outspoken, older and they didn't want to be bothered. I observed the way they interacted with each other, and the way they treated me, I tried to be a better person, you just can't please everyone. My first tutor was named Win. He was a short Chinese guy who knew a lot. Neither he nor anyone else wanted to teach me, but it was his job, so he capitulated. As appreciation, I tried not to be so overbearing. Weeks passed as I did my best to engage the material, but I learned slowly. Regardless of the speed I learned I remained dedicated, most of my time I was found in the math tutoring area. The students were much younger than I; but I didn't pay much attention to that, I only knew that many of the young ladies looked good, they were easy to talk to also. I usually stayed glued to my seat listening to Win. On several occasions he reminded me to stay focused on my work. After failing my remedial math class, I didn't want a repeat performance. I couldn't remember a time in my life that my grades had sunk so low.

From time to time a beautiful Dominican young lady came in the center seeking help with her math. I noticed her whitish complexion, like Morticia from *The Addams Family*. She was always so jubilant saying things at random, I liked her style for one girl so dedicated and hard working. I heard her say that she was receiving money in her bank account, not knowing exactly who was responsible for the deposits. Also, when she entered the room at times, she seemed like she could barely afford a whole meal. I saw her snacking on a few tidbits here and there. I even offered her some food, but she declined. I heard her say to another that she worked at TJ Maxx in the Wall Street area, that she gets off late and sometimes she's afraid to go home by herself at that time in the night. So, I went home and thought about her for a minute, then I asked my sister if I could borrow $10; I then fixed her some food I made and proceeded to go to the TJ Maxx store where she said she worked.

When I entered the store, I was amazed by the wide variety of things that they sold. I looked around to see if I saw her; she was daintily placing items on their respective racks. I slowly approached her, as she looked surprised. At first, she was happy to see me, then I explained to her that I was there to give her some food and the ten dollars I borrowed. The look of joy turned to one of disdain. She wanted absolutely nothing to do with me. I turned back around and left. Don't know if I thought of anything on my way home, but the train ride was quick, so I went to my room and mulled around till I fell asleep.

The next day I went to the school and was met by the security; they ushered me into a room on the side and told me I couldn't go in right now and that I was suspended. They notified me of a hearing I was to attend; that I was charged with stalking, and sexual harassment.

A few days had passed when I finally met the accuser at the hearing. The tribunal was a rinky-dink corn-ball sham of a witch hunt, biased in the accuser's favor. She told them some horrific lies that I had been trying to get with her on more than one occasion. There was seated a room full of funky big-legged women, and one dotard butt kiss man. They looked at me as though I was a monster. I don't think I have ever been so humiliated and disgusted in all my life. After they read off the charges to me, they brought her in; bowing and kowtowing like I really did something to her, then they went through the motions of giving me a fair hearing. The fact was they had made up their minds long before I came in the room in accordance with her testimony, deciding to suspend me, kick me out of school and derail my education. When it was all said and done, the school did what it was designed to do. As a black man, I felt the hatred and bias they had for me, even though the decision they made was based on a pack of lies spun by a lying opportunist.

Later, that day I went to my room at my sister's house and thought about what I was going to do. The mail had come, and I received a letter from the President, Barack Obama. He thanked me for sharing my story I wrote to him about me being in an abandoned building, while trying to sleep with multiple rats rifling through the garbage. I felt better when I read it; he has always been an inspiration. When I was working at Wendy's in 2008, I would work all day, then go out to canvas to support his campaign. I never thought about doing it for him because he was a black candidate. I only liked the message he had for all the people. He was such a fine person.

The tide had turned and once again and I was at odds with myself. I could never have thought my actions would have brought me to this position. At some moments I sulked thinking of my plight, the only thing I could do was fight the allegations thrust upon me. I reached out to a good friend who was a lawyer, he advised me to come to his office and he helped me develop a stratagem for my case. It seemed a little tedious at first to go over everything that had to be addressed for my response. Being older, I should have thought about the implications of me trying to talk to or getting involved with a younger student. If only I had children or raised some, my feelings probably would have been different, these things always were oblivious to me till now. I felt like a mindless oaf out of touch with reality. I learned from my mistake and was able to see what other people expected of me as an older gentleman.

I contacted my friend James Hubbard, the lawyer who constantly helped me place my ducks in a row. I would email him with the things he told me to write, and he would correct me till we had it hammered out. After we went over it, he was confident that we would have a positive result. The hearing was set for a few weeks after the incident. It was held at the CUNY office by Grand Central Station close to where I used to frequent as a messenger many years earlier. Not much had changed since I used to make my deliveries to some of the buildings; things were still top notch and elaborate. I arrived at the office on the ground floor. There was a security desk flanked with older employees who looked as though they had been at the helm for many years. When I entered through the door, they remained calm then asked me about my business I was there for. I told them about the hearing, and they looked up my case on the computer. A few minutes later I was escorted upstairs in the building and seated outside a hearing room. As I waited, Mr. Hubbert and a few of his colleagues came in and sat next to me then I was asked if I was nervous, he gave me some pointers. Finally, they called the case, and it was time for me to present it. The accuser didn't even show up; she must have felt embarrassed about the story she lied to these people about.

I began a methodical dissection of the events leading up to the day, speaking of my character. I gave them a picture from my niece's son Evan who had drew it while he was in school. It spoke of what he liked to do when he had free time on a day off, which was to be with his uncle Johnnie. To me this was a wonderful thing to say, so I gave the picture to the board so they could see the picture. As they examined it, I continued to speak about my quest to achieve my education. Towards the end I mentioned the letter I had gotten from the President. As they examined the letter it said that he was proud of me and my accomplishments. I also told them of the time my brother-in-law was reported as dying in the hospital; feeling the grief and despair I still gathered my books and went to the college, as to the testament of my dedication to receive my education; even though I was filled with grief I still went on my journey to my college. Then after the incident hearing that he was still alive, the joy it brought to my heart. I stood there for a long moment trying to compose myself on the brink of sobbing. Lastly, I explained the reason I thought the accuser did what she did, that the course was too hard for her to complete with the heavy burden of working in conjunction with going to the Pre-Calculus class. I told them she had gotten herself in trouble and was looking for an easy way out to be excused, a way to avoid flunking the course. I told them it was close to impossible to work those number of hours and satisfactorily complete the class. Maybe if she was in another school in a different situation, she may have done it, but not at our college; the work was just too demanding. After the hearing, they told me they will decide and will let us know.

I went home and waited for them to go through the process. Days passed knowing I did my best made me okay with whatever they decided. While waiting I began to reflect on all the events that led up to my expulsion. Thinking of an old saying made famous by the lovely Judge Judy: "Let no good deed go unpunished." I thought about the days in prison looking out through the cell bars; the mornings I woke early to be at Wendy's to open the store. Nothing I did seemed to be worth anything. I had to always kiss somebody's ass just to stay afloat. I wanted to get the respect of acquiring a degree. Education is the key to leaving poverty behind and living like a normal human being. It is the key to that better life that many of us seek and just can't grasp because of the chains and shackles society forces on us. I will never forget when I wanted to go to Brooklyn Tech High School; because of the criteria I couldn't attend because I didn't live in the right zip code, or should I say the *white* zip code. How much of a difference could it have made to go to school to be what I wanted to be, instead of whatever they allowed me to be? That one action made the difference of me being an engineer, scientist, or a jailbird; just one of the many obstacles that would present itself in my journey through life.

Mr. Hubbert called early that afternoon and said that I should meet him at his office. I spiffed up myself then took to the bus to the train station. It was still early while few people were riding so I had room to stretch out if I wanted to. I would usually put on my headset and listen to my classical songs, or whatever tickled my fancy on that day. There have been times when I sang a song or two while riding the subway. Since I liked to sing most people enjoyed a free moment of self-expression. I didn't charge money for my performances though, I only hoped people enjoyed what I did. Sometimes I got a favorable response, which I respected other people's opinion of me. It was a joy to give others a moment of happiness, a part of me that was deeply embedded in my soul.

Mr. Hubbert's office was Downtown Manhattan, a few blocks from Chinatown. When I went there, he told me he had my decision from the school board. Then he handed it to me as I read it slowly. They had decided to allow me to come back to school, under certain conditions. That I have nothing further to do with the accuser, neither could I involve anyone else in the falling out. I had to complete a Sexual Harassment Training course and not get in any more trouble while I attended classes. If I completed the next year without incident, they would expunge the charge from my school records. I agreed to the conditions, and I went back to school. When I saw her in the tutoring sessions, I acted as if I never knew her from before. I don't know how she felt about what she did to me, nor did I care. I wanted to be as far away from her as I could. Many people from third world countries have little or no regard for other human beings, that's why they are so unscrupulous. From then on in I remained reluctant to approach the ladies at the school, or even outside of it. I set some rules for myself to help me get through the remaining time. Staying to myself was one of them; not drinking and smoking was automatically understood as a no-no. Many others got caught up in that trap by trying to go to school and have a social life or be in toxic relationships. Being in college is really demanding, it requires one to make serious rational decisions that could affect the outcome of whether one graduates or not.

My routine was simple; I woke up, prayed to Allah, ate breakfast, took my medicine then headed for school. I paid close attention to what the professors were saying and did my homework. When I studied the prerequisites for the Rad-Tech program, I stayed in my room reading anatomy and physiology, at least two hours for every hour I spent in class. At the time, my goal of getting into that Rad-Tech program was the only thing I thought of. Sometimes I met women that I felt would be a nice lay, however I kept them at bay so I wouldn't get distracted. I went through my whole college years without getting a piece of ass. This is something that I'm not proud of but, it's the truth. I felt like such a loser at times; I would have paid for it if I could have, but I just couldn't. After a while I just became complacent by masturbating. I had to fantasize about something I should have been getting all along. I'm glad I didn't go around and sleep with any and every girl who came my way peddling her goods. Most of the women I would have been with were more interested in much younger guys with less ambitions; however, I sliced it I came out on top.

After taking prerequisites for two years, I came across an obstacle. I had this funny-style Mary Poppins professor that didn't exactly teach math the way I expected him to; he just wrote shit on the board and wanted you to figure it all out on your own. Most of the time I went to tutoring anyway so it didn't matter so much. We finally had a test with a three-variable problem; as most of the math was new to me, I struggled to get the correct answer. I went over it repeatedly till I had wasted most of the time allotted for the test. When it was all said and done, I failed the test. His sorry ass asked the class if anyone wanted to drop the class before we proceeded to the end of the semester. That way we could have had a chance to get a better grade later. I wanted to continue and not give up, after all I had a lot of motivation, I would have never thought of that as an option. So, at the end of the term, he gave me a D. A D for dumb, how unbelievable. Also, about this time I was scheduled for a meeting with the head of the Rad-Tech Dept. to see if I could get in the Radiological Technology program. I went in the room which she had set up with all her prospective students. They were foreigners from many different countries, mostly the Dominican Republic. Anyway, there was a girl that didn't speak very good English whom I helped occasionally with the Anatomy and Physiology material; she was placed in the class among all the other foreign students. She told me because I got a D I could not get in the program with a D in math. So, I took the class over in the summer to improve my grade, but she said I was too late because she already had the students for the next class. Then I learned that she let in a Russian guy after she told me no. I was flustered. After two years of taking all those prerequisites just to be told I can't do what I came to do, I couldn't believe this was happening to me. The effect of the accuser followed me throughout my journey. Even though I won the case, they still wanted to hold me responsible for trying to woo the girl or trying to get some. After the winch lied on me right at the beginning of my college endeavor, now another bitter pill to swallow. Thank you so much "Butt Fuck America." Thank you for giving all the opportunities to these rotten miserable cock suckers from every run-down shit hole around the world, and excluding me from the "Apple pie, The American Dream." This land was built on the back of my ancestors who made all this fine great land possible; however any and every person that washes up on our shores, you people can find a way to give them untethered access to all our resources and I can't manage to find enough here to take care of a portion of my needs. Thanks again "Butt Fuck America." I wonder is this how the Jews felt in Egypt before they were freed from bondage.

My days became filled with hatred and animosity towards the school. Every day I saw the nepotism along with the comradery amongst my cohorts. No one could have imagined the struggle it was to stay in attendance to this blemished institution for which I previously had so much admiration. All the issues stemmed from the incident with my accuser and the staff was exacting punishment by wayward means, whatever it was, it was horrendous.

I switched over to a Liberal Arts curriculum to get a different degree, one in Liberal Arts which it was meaningless settling for just anything I could get. I had to take even more math classes on a much higher level, all the way up to Calculus which was a big waste; my heart wasn't in it anymore. I also took physics at the same time in hopes of getting the degree quicker. Thank God for my friend Michelle; he was a genius from Haiti and very smart. He had a way of teaching math that made complicated things seem so simple. He brought me through most of my levels of math which I know I couldn't have made without him. My Calculus teacher was a joke. His name was Ginsburg, a real prick. I went to his office a few times for help, and he just yelled at me for not knowing some of the material. I believed he had ulterior motives, I wanted to smack the shit out of him before I remembered where that attitude might lead to. I stopped going to him for help; relying totally on Michelle who was sufficient in his mastery of transferring the concepts of his knowledge. I must admit the things they were teaching were not what I expected them to be, there was always a twist and turn to the methods which for some strange reason were never approached in my former years of learning.

Time moved slowly while I caught the eye of some of my classmates. At least two of them wanted to get next to me but I tried not to get involved. I noticed how so many students lost focus and quit school by getting into toxic relationships. I know I wanted to have sex with a few of those younger gals, but they looked at me differently than my younger peers, I guess I was just too old for them; most of them didn't have a problem with letting me know that either. When they did, I just fell back and continued my mission to graduate.

Going in the Hospitality Program was much more bearable and promising that the Rad-Tech program. I looked forward to being in my classes early in the morning, staying in school all day till it was time to go. I hardly did other things while I was attending, just the material for my classes. Whenever people had parties or social events I stayed away from that atmosphere. I knew from experience what that groove would lead to, or should I say that lifestyle.

The time was getting near for me to graduate, my goal was in sight, and I was ready to move to the next level. I started putting in applications for jobs and began looking into the possibilities of me working. I had been collecting disability payments from SSI. After going through a traumatic experience by the criminal justice system, I started getting these homicidal ideations of killing my so-called lawyer and the police officer who had arrested me for selling drugs. It was pitiful to see the level the criminal justice system had to stoop to get bodies to fill the beds in up-state prisons. The shitty police officer asked me to buy drugs for him; thinking I would get some when I bought them. He turned right around and arrested me for acting in concert to sell crack. The real person who was selling the drugs was a guy from the Dominican Republic, who had given another guy the drugs to sell so he could and make a few bucks. I was in the neighborhood after a three-day binder and saw the crackhead selling the stuff and thought I could get high too. I wound up spending two years in prison for this crime. That's how the law worked then, and I could never believe the system is fair working in the interest of Justice. It may be for some but not for me, especially at that time.

When I got out of prison in 1995, I was suffering from Post-Traumatic Stress Disorder (PTSD). That's when I applied for SSI under those circumstances. There were times I would envision myself killing the cop who had arrested me for selling drugs and my lawyer who was supposed to, that didn't represent me when I was sent upstate for the crime. That's the solution they came up with; to lock up all the crack heads and let the real dealers go, I guess this is the way they perpetuate their failing system. After all they had to fill up the beds to get federal dollars to pay for everything. They built these prisons not to just look at, but to fill them up, no matter who. So, I pursued the disability claim after years of going to Psyche doctors and making appointments. I didn't like the idea of me being categorized as someone that couldn't function right, but I was not playing with a full deck anymore I portrayed, especially after getting felony convictions on my arrest record, this handicapped me from getting a job. In the years long after society eased up the restrictions allowing people with felonies to gain employment.

When I graduated from my college, I earned a BA in Hospitality Management. I wanted to use my degree to get a decent job and start paying off my student loans. I went on an interview with Restaurant Associates to work at the Google building in Chelsea on 8th Ave and 14th Street. The district manager gave me a position as a line cook. I started working there and reaping the benefits immediately. I would leave my house about 4:30 A.M. to 5:00 A.M. to be there by 6:00 A.M. I started out in the basement in the production area. They had me prepping and baking chicken breast. I didn't like it so much because the supervisor was a nuisance. He would yell or bark intimidating the workers which were under extreme pressure to get the work done. He only knew he didn't want to answer to his superiors.

Most every morning I would get up and meet my neighbor's wife and kids by their car about 5:30 or so, she would take me to the train station. She was so nice and lovely; sometimes I wished I had a woman like her because she had so many good qualities. Even though I liked her so much I didn't try to come on to her, the reason being I was happy for her and her husband both; also, I wouldn't want another guy I trusted to come on to my wife, especially if she was so fine. I was happy they allowed me to see how they lived their life as a couple. They also had two children who were well mannered, I liked their whole family dynamics. I got to see what it was like for another black man to be successful in raising his family who was not at odds with the law or any other normal impediments of society. I looked at him and tried to use him as a model for good living and an example of a good life. His name is Darryl and his wife's name is Natasha. He was a descendant from the Southern Blacks, and she was from the West Indies. They had a special kind of love that I admired and one that they lived.

When I arrived at work, I was a little early most days, I was reminded not to punch in until the proper time. So then, some mornings I would be preparing my station, getting it ready for work or something related to work when my boss, my supervisor Duane McDonald would come in and remind me to not be working off the clock, even if I didn't punch in. I felt bad having to be told that, but I got the picture. He was such a nice guy, even though he was white I never felt anything that went along with that accolade. As far as I can say most of the staff at Restaurant Associates were fine decent people who did a fantastic job. For me, the job was better than any I held in all my life, including the one at Davis, Polk, and Wardwell. One of the things I liked so much was there was so many things that a person could have stolen if their head was into it; and nobody over them looking and peering from behind closed doors waiting to nab you if you did; of course. There was security watching everyone, but I for one didn't go to work to be a thief especially when anything I wanted was at my disposal. I loved being there with all those fine people from the moment I arrived till the end of the day when I went home.

There were two people who had taken a liking to me, but I was not interested. I only went there to do my job. You can tell when people like you, but these two were living in some alternate reality. I never meant to lead them astray, but they made me feel a bit uncomfortable. After a while Duane moved me upstairs to another position where I felt much more at ease in doing my work. When I complained about the level of the table, which made my back hurt, so he made an adjustment for me that made the difference, he gave me a table that was higher than the other ones, now I was ready to do my best.

At first, they had me making two types of peanut butter and jelly sandwiches: one with white bread and grape jelly, and the other with multigrain and strawberry jam. The clients went crazy for them, so I had to keep them in stock. Usually by the end of the day they were all gone from the Grab-and-Go compartment. There were other sandwiches I made from a recipe book that took a little refinement, just till I got them right. It took a while, but some people got used to them on a regular basis. I always tried to make them as if I were going to eat them myself. As I made my sandwiches there were other cooks making other things in the kitchen area. We all had our individual space to perform our operations. This was okay I guess for a while, then as time went on I thought about working at other stations. From time to time, I did; I guess this is the way I could have gained more experience and possibly advanced to another position paying more and having more responsibilities. Sometimes when I looked at the supervisor's performing tasks like going over the payroll or clocking me in with a correction of my hours it didn't look so easy, but I knew I could have done those operations also, if I had the training.

Most of the time I arrived early and stayed till it was time to go; then every now and then I was asked to stay late or work at another area. There was the deli station which I enjoyed because I got a chance to interact with the clients for whom paid my salary. They were pleasant 100% of the time. When I got the chance, I would overload their sandwiches like when I worked by Wall Street. There was a place I frequented quite often when I was younger, they made these fabulous, overstuffed sandwiches that gave me the idea to pile it on for the clients. How I loved the genoa salami and provolone with a half-sour pickle and a Coke. I would get my sandwich and go outside my building, 1 Chase Plaza and watch the people as I ate my lunch. When I first started working at the law firm, I would take my lunch in an area next to the mailroom where there was trash containers and debris waiting to be thrown out. I was shy I guess and didn't mingle too much with people on the job. Now that I think about it, this may have left the wrong impression; that I was waiting to go through the garbage for something to eat, I just never thought about it until I developed more social skills. I didn't care too much for idle chatter or pretending I was a friend to people when I didn't really know them. The boss would always find work for me when I spent time in that area. He would send me uptown with a few packages that were at stops so I could make money off. After a certain number of blocks I walked, I would get an extra token for carfare. This helped me out a lot when I first started working because I didn't have money for lunch every day.

The longer I stayed the better my situation became. Over the years of being there I transformed into a well-respected decent young man. I remember mornings I put at least fifty dollars in my pockets for my expenses, which didn't happen before Greg taught me the ropes. Greg was another older black guy there who was also into photography; he showed me how to get more money by an alternate means. I wasn't stealing, not exactly, just exaggerating on the receipts I turned in. I went from making about $167 a week to $375 to $450 at times. This enabled me to help my mother more. She would be so happy when I gave her extra money for whatever she needed. She would tell her friends, the few that she had nice things about me. The women in my neighborhood would look at me in awe as if I were something special. I was oblivious to their feelings, as I was not the kind to blow my own horn. I only know it felt good to please my mother and make her happy. She always gave me and my siblings joy. There were many days she sacrificed for us to give us the best she could. I can only imagine the drudgery of going to work leaving her children at night to provide as a single parent. My dad didn't help her at all when they separated, he only lived his life away from the rest of the family.

Having found my niche at Google via Restaurant Associates I met this young lady, Shannon Brown. She was cute, young and tender with a child already. I met her one day coming from Burger King with her baby. I had been reluctant on speaking to women for a while; going through a long dry spell. When I met her I asked her if it was okay to get her number, she asked me if she gave me her number would I appreciate her. I said I surely would. I called her soon after and took her out a few times. Then she told me her baby's daddy wanted to reconcile with her, so I backed off and let the cards fall where they may. Time passed and I saw her again by the bus stop by Brooklyn Hospital. We spoke and rekindled our friendship. I started talking to her again. I explained to her that whenever I deal with someone, I aim to make their life better than when I entered their life. I tried to do just that with her; I made her life better, but she did nothing but try to bring me down. I regret letting such an ungrateful person in my life and spending time with her and her child. It's because of her and people like her I stay to myself, or reluctant to let them have any part of me. The reason I say that is she asked me for money to help buy food for her and her family to eat over the holidays. To me I think you must be very desperate to ask people for money about that time. So, after I helped her she gave me her ass to kiss, while having sex with another dude. A guy who is a notorious weed head. I later heard out the two of them were making plans to get a car to drive for UBER. She was young and so was he. Thank you Lord for delivering me from that mess.

When I got her out the back door of my life, another sweet young lady, Winter, entered and fulfilled some of my needs. When I met her, she was talking about guys not trying to give up that bread. She was selling pussy by the hour and by the pound. She had some good stuff too and was devoted to her craft. She was always so pleasant and professional. I guess because I paid like I weighed. Shannon was trash and Winter was the treasure. The reason I say that is I did everything I could to make that trash bag happy; however, no matter what I did it was never enough for her. I took her out to eat at a lot of nice places; when we would leave them, she would save almost half of her meals for her family, always bringing a portion home for her poor broke household. She did me a big favor by leaving when she did. I can see myself as an unhappy individual living in constant misery if I had stayed with her. Or something worse might have happened, no telling. She didn't even have a birth certificate when I met her. I had to keep on top of her to get it, I also tried to motivate her to better her life and go back to school so she could get a good job and take care of herself and her crying ass baby, anyway life goes on.

About this time, my sister told me that she had gotten a buyer for her house and that she needed me to move out so she could sell it. I called around and asked a few people if they knew of any place that was available, I spoke to my friend who was my counselor previously at a program I went to called NRI on 37th Street in Manhattan. He told me that there was a room next to him on Miller Ave in the East New York section of Brooklyn. After applying for Section 8 and Public Housing in 2004, I was hoping that I would have gotten something by then. Most of the things I bought was in anticipation of one day having my own apartment. I went to check it out and thought it was okay for the price. The bathroom had curtains with black mold on it, I didn't pay any mind. The room was too small for all my possessions though, and it was not ideal for me, don't even know what made me take it, I guess it was the thought of my sister selling her house that made me take it so abruptly, and I thought I would be happy living by an old friend.

Not long after settling in, I spent time together with my old drug counselor; we traded stories of me when I was struggling with my addiction and his endeavors since I left. There weren't that many, so the conversation moved on to another thought. He started telling me about his daughter liking me and how she wanted to get with me. I had not thought much about her over the years that I'd known her, and I didn't know what to think of it. We would drink up some beers and I still had some bottles of liquor left in my room. When he drank, he became drunk and weird. I didn't know he couldn't hold his liquor. After belting down a few shots, he would turn into a backwoods, loudmouth, as if he just started drinking for the very first time in his life.

I awoke each morning as I had previously to moving in that room, somewhere about 4:30 A.M. to catch the train to the city. My stop was 14th Street and 8th Ave at the Google building. I would take the elevator up to my area; there were always snacks, coffee and breakfast foods in the canteens for the employees in case they got hungry while working. With these spaces filled with foods and drinks there was no need to go outside the building whenever an employee got hungry if they were working. I would usually take my breakfast in that area before I started, it didn't cost me anything. The floors were kept immaculate, and people always left their personal items strewn about, no one dared to touch them, at least I didn't. It was a dream come true to be all alone in a wide-open space with laptops, supplies, pens, notepads, and anything to make a dollar if you were that type. Maybe when I was using drugs or just desperate, I might have thought of taking a chance, but not when I had achieved the success of being in such a fine establishment. People like me always dreamed of having a job like this where there were such a fine class of people who were always friendly, kind and well to do. They never talked condescending to me or showed a side that they were better than. It was a culture of elation and an air of tranquility; most people I knew that worked there enjoyed being there partially because of the other co-workers and for what the Google values stood. Here it was me, a four-time felon, a college graduate who had been strung out on drugs to the point of being homeless, working in one of the best places in America. I loved every day that I was there in the servitude of such a fine class of people, one that gave me a second chance and didn't discriminate against me for my past.

I did well there for a while, a long while. I had become acclimated with the recipes of the sandwiches that I made, and the clients loved them. When I came into the prep areas in the mornings, there would be water on the floor from the dishwasher machine; I would mop it up then gather my utensils. I might check the clock and prepare my area for my daily assignment. Once I clocked in, I would make my sandwiches and complete my task. If I finished quick enough, I would help my co-workers. They always had job openings in case I wanted to work elsewhere, also they promoted a lot from within. Sometimes I enjoyed working at other stations, what I liked most was giving the clients the best service I could give them. Years ago, when I worked by Wall St. there was a thing called Over-Stuffed sandwiches. I recreated that at Google; the sandwiches I made were Super-Overstuffed which I hoped the clients enjoyed as much as I did making them. Sometimes the clients would ask me not to put in so much meat or other ingredients. But for the ones that allowed me to create their fantasy, it was a wonderful experience. They were coming back, hoping I was there to indulge them. As I say to you, what I said to them, the pleasure was all mine.

When I was finished for the day, I had to make sure my station was cleaned and sanitized. It took a few minutes to make sure things were in order; then I would call my manager to give the place the once over. Then upon their approval I was free to go home. To think I started this job while living at my sister's house and now I was away from her and my family trying to make it on my own again. Living in East New York was no thrill for the simple fact that there weren't many others like me working a nine-to-five under similar circumstances. I had been up and down so many times under the grips of drugs and finally managed to go to school and get a degree. After achieving that goal, I secured an exceptionally decent job that I loved more than any other. For some strange reason, the things that mattered so much in the past had disappeared, as far as me being a black man with a criminal past; at Google it just didn't matter, this made me work even harder to prove myself and give the absolute best service I could. I can't say for sure, but I believe President Trump may have had something to do with me being able to get a job at such a fine place. It was like he told white people to hire more blacks regardless of their circumstances. Maybe or maybe not, it didn't matter anymore, I was simply happy to be able to work a job and pay my way; this was so important to me to feel like I had some value.

Everything was fine for a while, then I started allowing people to weasel their way in my life. First it was a guy named Snake who was always by the train station. He was a dope-head that knew where the good stuff was. He seemed to live right there at that train station because whenever I came home or went to work, he was there to sponge or leech something from me. I started slowly backsliding into the drug scene; from my well-established position, one led to two and two led to hell. It took a while, but I lost a lot of what I accumulated: many of my possessions, my dignity, respect and finally my job. It didn't happen overnight, I was just so dumb, I guess. I mixed up with the low-class people that wanted nothing more in life but to get high or just barely enough to survive. It was a real treat for them to have me in their circle; I always had money and they just wanted to leech off me, everybody only wanted to get some of what I had. It took time for me to learn that they meant me no good at all. I had to pay my dues again because I never learned to sever the umbilical cord from the low lives and vagabonds.

I would work all day then get high all night, not get any sleep then go to work the next day; come home and continue where I left off. This went on for a while maybe a few times in a week. As it went on I became less interested in my daily routines and started an anything goes approach to my life-style. When I first moved into my room I filled up my space with my possessions. I really exceeded the space limit, not having enough room to turn around or breathe. There were times when I'd go to reach for something and things from other places in my room would fall. Late at night when I'd be trying to rest I'd get visits from mice scrounging around for food. I might have cooked earlier in my room, and they'd smell the remnants of what I had. There were also roaches that didn't seem to mind a few crumbs scattered along the floor. In this summer, I didn't have too many problems with mosquitoes or flies; it seemed that the overall population of these two creatures had dwindled through the years. With global warming rising, plenty of things didn't behave the way they used to. The whole ecosystem seemed off kilter while the politicians debated the conjecture. As a concerned citizen I naturally wanted to help resolve the issues that would help prolong our symbiotic relationship with the planet. However, this has been an issue out of the average person's hand. Many of us wonder if the trajectory we are headed will afford the next generations the same opportunities to enjoy nature the way we did. My mother used to tell me to "have look back for others." In other words, to have consideration for other people. Make the necessary changes to correct global warming, (Plant more trees, utilize more solar power, less carbon and methane emissions, everyone work together to save our planet).

It might have been about 4:30 A.M. when I left my house for the train to the city. At that time in the morning, I thought about the robbers in the neighborhood; fortunately, I was only two blocks away from the subway. There were usually crackheads and dope fiends out on the street. Sometimes they would be lucky enough to ask you for something. If you had it and you felt like giving it you would, if not you didn't.

As I came home from work my room door would sometimes be ajar. I wondered if I was that absent minded to have left it like that. Also, I noticed things in my room slightly out of place, or just missing. Coupled with the fact of using drugs my issues were not as big as how to get the next one. It would be nighttime, and I would have the urge to get high, especially if I had a few drinks with the neighbor/ex-counselor/so called friend. My eyes would be on the clock, and when I had cut off the get high time to get some sleep so I could go to work. Sometimes I would be so tired, I'd have to drink a beer before I rode the train was a usual response. I didn't tell the people on my job what I was going through, but they could see I was losing a grip on life. My clothes weren't so dirty, but they began to smell funny. People noticed some changes in me but gave me the benefit of the doubt. One girl who had a family member that used drugs recognized the signs I displayed but was still cordial; she chose not to come right out and boldly blow up the spot by accusing me of using drugs to my face. Instead she just remained distanced. Perhaps she could have been the positive influence I desired, the rhythm of a sweet hot tamale. For quite a while I gave her subtle hints I was interested, but no matter those cards weren't gonna be played on her tally board. Not for anything the head supervising chef had been lining her up, and she was receptive. In the corporate world it's not always what you know that helps you rise to better positions.

It was still summertime now, and my endurance had worn mighty thin; it was hard to keep getting high while trying to work. The chef had gave me several warnings about the no call-no-shows I had accrued; she said if I continued this pattern of insubordination, she would have no other choice but to take the appropriate action. In a way I was hoping they would fire me because I no longer deserved to be a part of the team. I had got high that night and was home asleep when I woke up and realized I was late again, not wanting to bother with work. I called her and she told me to come in anyway. When I arrived, she told me I was to go to a special meeting she had arranged. This was the last day for me to grace the halls of the Google building. I had my hearing and was finally getting what I deserved, a nice big fat termination after all the unnecessary bullshit I put the job through. The chef asked me for my security badge, and I was escorted to the exit. I went downstairs into the subway to the A train for the ride home. This was sort of the end of the world for me. I felt a great sense of loss, everything I had worked for in the past few years had been dissolved, as if I hadn't accomplished anything at all in that span of time. I knew this would happen, but I just didn't know when. I had to gather my thoughts about what I was gonna do. I know I wanted to leave that area; the room I had become a source of bad memories. The people in the neighborhood seem to cast condescending eyes on me and my disgraceful fall from grace. I only knew most of them from a distance, from me coming and going to work.

I concluded that I would put my stuff back in storage and move from there. My funds were low, so I cashed in my insurance policy that I had for my sister. I took the money and rented a truck which my brother drove for me, because I never really learned to drive. We took everything out of the room, and I hung around the area for a while, perhaps a few weeks before I made up my mind to go through the shelter system again.

I started out at the main shelter called Bellevue on 30th St and 1st Ave in Manhattan. A few days later I was at Bedford and Atlantic Ave in Brooklyn, they call it Castle Greyskull like in the He-Man cartoon. After a few weeks I was transferred to another shelter in Flatbush called Kingsborough; it was on Clarkson and Albany Ave. Then I was transferred to another one on Chauncey and Broadway, then to Bob's Place in Jamaica, then the Red-Carpet Inn in Jamaica Queens. At the end of a two-year transition period, I was placed in a 4th floor walkup on 151st and St Nicholas Ave in Manhattan. I had to share the bathroom with other residents, while in my room mice ran ramped in the night, some of the residents continuously threw debris on the floors in the hallway and kept the place in a state of dilapidation.

After being there for an extended time I put in for a transfer. It wasn't so easy, but my case was exceptional. I had arthritis in my knees, developed heart disease, which made it difficult for me to navigate the stairs. The guys from the area hung out in our building smoking weed, acting as if they paid rent there making the residents that did lived there lives difficult. I had to share the bathroom with people that would always find a reason to throw trash somewhere on the floors of common areas. Mice frequently invaded my room in the nighttime scrounging around for food, hoping to find a tasty morsel with no regard for me or my need for sleep. There was one mice that came in and woke me with the noise, when I looked up it was swinging, dangling navigating its way up my speaker which was covered in a felt cloth. I wanted to take a spoon or shoe and crack it upside its little head, but I was just too tired to move, so I just laid there hoping I could manage to get back asleep. The other residents may have also kept food around for them inadvertently. It was in the best interest for everyone to allow me to change my housing now. I asked my caseworker to assist me to move out of those conditions. She looked over my case got approval and put me in for the transfer. Being that I paid my rent-on time and having an effective doctor's note helped a lot with the process. condition began one winter day, when I had slipped on some ice and snow by my sister's house; I fell back on both my knees, tearing the cartilage and ligaments I guess. When I had my knees examined the X-ray report made me aware of this issue to be an ongoing problem. Climbing stairs or running would become more difficult as I became older unless I had it corrected.

I was given a listing of potential renters and agents in the metropolitan area. There were a substantial number of contacts that appeared in this listing, however when I applied for something that I thought I would like, there was always an issue. I would call a number and speak to a person at their company, when I tried to further the applications, the person that I initially spoke to would not answer again. It was as though they knew I was a black guy from my voice and resigned to offer anymore assistance. Other times I would email they person or agent and inquire if they take the CityFHEPS voucher, they will stop responding. This went on quite a few times, then I stopped applying. These individuals were trying to fill their units with a particular kind of people, of which I was not included. I went on countless interviews in the past years, and it was always the same excuse, you make too much or too little, or anything lame to preclude me from the opportunity. I surely had my fill and decided to go back to the shelter system. I hated that more than anything, but I knew I stood a better chance if I had an active case. I waited from 2004 to get in the Section 8 program; I had an interview in 2009 for my application and was told I was not eligible because my brother-in-law didn't pay a schedule F tax. They held me responsible for my brother-in-law's actions, and when I appealed the decision I was still denied. I could have come from another country halfway around the world, with no ties to this country and received housing assistance from the Downtown Brooklyn office, but for an American black man it was close to impossible to get help. One of the reasons they gave was that I was on the waiting list for public housing.

After exhausting my legal remedies, I proceeded to file a federal case of discrimination in the Eastern District Court. I asked to have my hearing by a jury and to proceed as a poor person. The judge that was assigned to the case took almost a year to decide whether to allow me to proceed as a poor person; when she finally decided for me to proceed, she started asking me for more information about the case, which I explained to her in the statement of facts that my file was destroyed, that the records in the (FOIL) unit, had been corrupted. It was as if she already made up her mind not to do anything about it, long before the case was in her possession. She found every excuse in the world not to move forward with the case. She had made up her decision long before she even got it. That is how the law is working in the courts of today. The most sneaky, underhanded, shifty individuals are now in control of the courts, so don't waste your time with them trying to resolve an issue. If you want justice, you may have to hold court in the streets.

As the years went by, the decisions they made helped to create extremely volatile living conditions here in the city. So many black children growing up in poverty, parents on drugs, fathers in jail, getting involved with gangs made it almost impossible for the average citizen to live a decent life. We all must ask what role we played in the scenario; how did our hand help contribute to making living in New York City unbearable. The crime rate has increased very quickly, with people sleeping in the streets, judges and politicians taking money who accepted no culpability as our society spiraled out of control. Jackass judges and lawyers twisted the laws to the point that it became unsafe for anyone to leave their households. If a person committed a very serious offense today, they might be back roaming the streets that night. Seemed like it mostly happened in black neighborhoods. I don't like to be perceived as a racist, but we may all be guilty of it to some degree, especially living under these extreme conditions. I wouldn't wish that accolade on my worst enemy. It's not a wish though it has become a stark reality in the world we live in today. Many of the residents are afraid to leave their houses in fear of the criminal elements that prowl the streets. We don't even know if we will make it back to our homes safely. I've never seen anything like what is going on today. Seems like there are no solutions that help alleviate our issues. Average people's lives are becoming less of value. It's not just black people randomly killing others for no good reason, it's that some individuals have the upper hand, and they may get away with it. Perhaps they don't enjoy the drudgery of life's ups and downs and they seek a quick solution where they can live in a closed environment where they don't have to work for anything. Some want the benefit of being in a jail or lock up. It can't be the notoriety because there is always someone in there that's badder than you. I am starting to believe that the ones who commit these acts are not even human. How could they be? They must be a sub-human species that have infiltrated humanity; a set of demons that have evolved to the human plane. They should be erased immediately once they show their true colors. If we take severe actions and take away the chance of living the life of Riley behind closed doors in our prisons, things could change. It is a great idea if when someone goes on a random killing spree for no reason, they should be snuffed out right there on the spot, no more 15 minutes of fame. I remember when these Looney Tunes first started going on these killing sprees how the media would plaster their stories in the news, all day on every channel the same story. If we paid less attention to them, perhaps they may try to cope differently. Today a large part of society has chosen to take on these unsavory tactics; many perpetrators randomly commit unspeakable acts without any fear of reciprocity. Another amazing aspect of the law is when those who are in control of the judicial system finds out that they may have put someone behind bars by mistake, wrongly accused, unjustly punished for a crime they did not commit, there is no culpability. No sorry, no compensation, no nothing on the part of the system in most cases. I feel judges should be held responsible for these disgusting acts of cruelty, especially if they weren't diligent in preserving the rights of the defendants as well as getting the facts straight. They should be jailed just like the person they put in jail or prison. They don't need to be in such an important position when they don't want to do their job; perhaps take a short cut for easy convictions. Everyday black folk send their children to school to in of getting an education; instead, their being bogged down with crowded classrooms where many of the students don't come to learn but are being vetted for gangs and subversive tactics. While some kids come to learn many of our children are there for a fashion show. It's not what you know but, what kinds of clothes you have on, or how much drugs you're selling, or Tik Tok challenges they can do. The level of math and English being taught here are substandard to other third world nations. The things students learn in a junior high school in other countries they teach us in our colleges. We are being set up to lose, the system is designed to fail; without proper guidance we may be lost.

Most every junction of their precious lives, an obstacle is being placed by an overwhelming racist, unfair system that perpetuates poverty, death, and destruction. Some leaders think they know everything, no one does and what they do know, not many will find out because they discriminate or treat some better than others. As you may or may not see it has a toll on all of us; we all pay for the actions of those in charge. So, when and if a person finally manages to get a decent job, they will be only working to pay the rent, anything extra is a blessing, and yet there is no governmental actions to rectify this or representation of the people who have to live under these conditions, work all week so somebody else can benefit off our labor. If black folk ever want to get out of this rut, we should break free of the chains, and shackles of this society, we must work together to be a free nation, we must have unity. Seems as if they keep killing off all our leaders, but we need to be unified for this nightmare to end. We can't allow anyone else to do it for us, we must do it ourselves. Our black people must be sick and tired of so many others that wash up on our shores, that come to this land and make it, achieve success, the American dream and we as a people are always stuck on the bottom, like a piece of gum on a shoe. It is very hard for people to navigate through a system where most everyone is against you, and those in choice positions deliberately place obstacles in your way to ensure you never make it. There are some sick and seditious people in this world; whose only desire is to cause chaos. I don't want our children to always have to struggle all their lives to have nothing; to only manage to achieve what others will allow us to. We have some very serious issues, extremely bad habits. There is a lack of help and unity for each other, we are quicker to destroy one another than to help. This is not the way to be if we want to get ahead. With climate change we must think about our future. Where are we gonna be when the shit hits the fan? Who will we turn to? Things can get ugly if we let it.

The time is now to put on our big person pants and stop wandering through life aimlessly allowing other people to dictate our outcomes. Consider the children, do they love us today, do they respect us? The answer is no; it's hard to love someone that does not love and care for themselves. There is so much animosity in the younger generation towards older folk, in many instances they are opposed to their elders. The truth is older people let them down as they were brought into a society believing that life is fair; that they had a good chance to make it and live the so-called American Dream if they played by the rules, this is a lie. There are too many others who have a vested interest in seeing blacks fail. From the time I grew up in this city obstacles were deliberately placed in my path. When I first decided to go to Brooklyn Tech High School, to be something else or another kind of student I was told, I couldn't go there for this reason: it was my zip code. When I tried to get into the military service with the Air Force, they wouldn't accept me because they wanted copies of my medical records from when I was a child. After working at the law firm for four years as a messenger, they decided to give raises to two other workers who were in the same shoes as I; we were hired all about the same time but for me there was no promotion, only a stick of butter to grease my ass after they finished fucking me. The girl I loved and wasted the better part of a year, riding far and deep into unknown neighborhoods trying to find her, spending endless hours wondering if I would ever see her again, dumped me because she didn't believe in me anymore, and the vestige of my past. After losing such a tasty morsel, my desire for other women diminished more, and more over time. Perhaps I felt that I wasn't getting my just due. The thrill was gone leaving little to be desired. Even though I've been with many other women over the years, I still carried a flame in my heart for her, a heart that is cold and lifeless, like a dead flower that has been forsaken, one that doesn't receive any water or nourishment. The only jobs I found seemed like they were all entry level with no future. Drugs and alcohol seemed to find its way in every low-class neighborhood. The friends I had dwindled down to the lowest of the lows. Just couldn't catch a break, no matter how hard I tried, so much so that I gave up or I found myself fighting a losing battle. This is Butt Fuck America, a place where I have no place as far as this society is concerned. The only place this country seems to have for me is doing something at odds with society to achieve my dream, selling drugs, non-taxed cigarettes, robbing people, stealing from others, screwing my close friend's woman. Every subversive, wicked, no-good way is always an option, one that I don't want. So, until I catch a break doing something that is legal and righteous I'll stay broke or try to find a way to get the things I like legally.

When I was deeply engrossed in my addiction, I wondered if I will ever break free from the grips of the drugs and alcohol. Didn't happen overnight, it just took most of my good years away; this is something that I want to relay to the youth of today. Don't waste your time getting buzzed and having a good time, do what the other people from other nations do who come here, work and save your cash, stay out of trouble, and take care of your families. Stay away from all that "Tough Tony" stuff, focus and find like-minded individuals who want to live a happy normal life.

Some mornings I woke up hungry, regretting not saving a dollar or to buy breakfast or something to put in my belly. I'd lay on my sister's couch or a spot somewhere inside there and somebody would knock on the door. They wanted somebody to cop for them or they had already copped and needed a place to smoke. They might ask me to go for them and that would be the beginning of my run, off to the races. A run can last a few days because I was never satisfied. Throughout the journey I could land anywhere. When the high wears off, usually after a few days of running, my body would be extremely tired. My feet would be so sore that they could scream. The drugs could help that feeling and send me right back out for a few more days, but if I had a little volition, I would not take that next one. One time I went on a mission for about fourteen days straight. I don't know how but I did it; once my sister-in-law found me standing up asleep leaning on a traffic meter, or a mailbox, it was such a long time I can't remember which. Sometimes I enjoyed the high, it made me feel special, other than. One of the things I did was go into abandoned buildings to take a blast. After I did, I would sometimes start looking at the floor for crumbs or rocks that I thought I lost. We call that ghost-busting, looking for something that isn't there. The places were places where people had previously lived, and they left. Each had their own reason for leaving but when I walked through them the places had items in them I could sometimes sell to get more crack or alcohol. There might also be things that I might want to keep for myself. I have found, lost, and squandered so many treasures through the years. When I found something good, people tried to give me whatever they wanted for it. For me that wasn't gonna work. I would rather keep walking until I got a good price for things if I could. Or sometimes I settled for less to get a quick fix. I was in Flatbush one day and I managed to find my way to Debbie's house, I wanted to find out why I had been plagued with so many calamities in my life if there was some esoteric meaning why I had to suffer endlessly after our lives crossed paths. I rang her doorbell, but no one came and acknowledged me, so after a few minutes I left. I began to walk scratching my head, hoping that Debbie never found out about that moment, wondering why she meant so much to me and why I didn't let it go. If there was a reason that I obsessed over her, perhaps to me she was a dream come true. Why did life ruin me and my chances? Sometimes it was never the same feelings without the one you hoped for, the one you dreamed would come your way and it all gets ruined.

After walking for about half an hour I entered a supermarket, looking for something to steal and sell. I picked up some steaks and tried to hide them under my shirt. After I left the store the security followed me and began to chase me. As I ran away I flung the individual packs of meat in the air. By the time he caught up to me, I was all out. He looked around mad as hell that I didn't have any left and the ones I had thrown down, people were picking them up as he looked on, then he ran back quickly to retrieve the ones he could.

Some days I could go in a building while it was still light outside and when I finished it hanging around inside it would be dark. Some people would look at me and give me the eye, saying inwardly, "Look at that crackhead, he's high now." I'd just go about my business hoping I could scrounge up enough change for a beer to take the heebie-jeebies off me. Of the best places to beg for change was at a fast-food restaurant. One of my favorite places was Kentucky fried chicken. People often gave more change there and they also asked if I was hungry and buy me food. I did a lot of other things to get money to; one was steal from trucks parked at a light. I would walk up behind the back and see if it was unlocked. I would then open it and grab what I could before the light changed. Then I would walk off with the items and sell them to the nearest buyer. I was in the city once and I had hopped on the back of a truck, while it was moving somebody from another car alerted the driver, he stopped, and I jumped off the back while he got out of the truck to see what was going on. After he went back in his truck, I jumped on again and the truck reached a good speed, maybe about 50 mph, and somebody told him that there was somebody back there. This time he saw me and gave me a warning, "Don't be screwing around."

Sometimes I came off with some very good items which varied from job to job. When I did this I worked alone; the first robbery I did with two other guys, and I didn't like the feeling. Some poor old man going home I guess, walking down Broadway by himself. I grabbed him and the other guys ran his pockets. When we finished, they told me that they didn't get anything. Also, I didn't like the way the guy felt when I held him at bay, some would call it a strong-arm robbery, also I felt used, so I never did that again. I chose to go a different way from then on I didn't like doing anything with other black guys, this sounds sad because I'm black. The problem is we don't all think alike. I was always better off by my lonely. I could go out on a mission and get high as a kite and stay for days managing all my needs by myself. Even though I stayed out there on the streets for most of the time I could never find fulfillment, I always seemed to be incomplete. One of the saddest feelings I dealt with was I felt so unwanted. I would see others that were worse off than me who had women or girlfriends that were theirs, they stuck with their dope-fiend counterparts, perhaps I was a bit jealous but more surreal it made me feel kind of worthless. It wasn't self-pity or putting myself down, I knew I could do better in life, I just had to concentrate and put my mind to it. There were plenty of times I went out and found women that hung for a while, but they never seemed to want to stay. Some of them were looking for more amenities, more than I could provide, others went their separate ways. This makes me think that there was something I was doing wrong if I wanted to keep women in my life. I guess I tried to play the good guy role most of the time, this just didn't get me anywhere, women don't respect good guys. They can be puzzling among other things; the truth is I don't want to figure anything out. No matter what I do there is always something wrong and I am tired of trying. I find me being alone has helped immensely with my peace of mind. Of course, I want the trappings of having a good companion, someone to do for and vice versa, but I just don't see it in the near future, it may take a while. Perhaps if I hadn't gone through so much crap to find and be with one I might feel differently. But for now, I'll keep waiting till the day comes.

As I wait I've gotten older, my days are shorter and the only thing that sticks with me is the time I had with my mom. My dear beloved mother, who fought so hard to instill her values in her children. She knew a lot about life, though she was not rich and famous. She was so poor, always giving her last to raise us. She didn't spend her money buying things for herself, no new clothes, shoes, not much of anything for herself. If she had a dime she saved it for her children in case they needed it. She worked and raised nine heads by herself.

I remember all the times she spent with us, how she took us to schools, gave us money throughout the year, even for Christmas, and went on picnics at Central Park. She also fed poor people who were strangers, and she sang when she was happy.

Somehow I got hooked on drugs (crack and alcohol). One time I wanted some money from her to get high with and she told me no. I reminded her of the money I gave her when I was working at Davis Polk. She just looked at me, and she didn't say a word. After all, she has done for me in my life, that's how I repaid her, trying to make her feel guilty about taking the money I gave her; what was I thinking? If I could have taken back those words it would have meant so much, but it's too late now, she's gone. The joy of my life has left me, knowing how sick I was, knowing what I'd become. She begged me, pleaded with me to get off that stuff I just couldn't help myself. I wasn't clean then, but I'm clean now, Mom. I know I owe you; it wasn't supposed to end like that. You were here with me, and then you were gone. I couldn't achieve one good thing in time before you left, one thing to make you proud again. The only thing I can give you is me living life without using drugs. Thanks for everything Mom, I love you.